# *find your* HAPPY

## PLANNER

## THE ROAD TO RECLAIMING YOUR AUTHENTIC LIFE

♥

**RHONDA ZARATE**

Rhonda Zarate www.rhondazarate.com

First Printing, 2016

ISBN 978-0-9952216-0-4

Design by Nicole Rinaldi www.innov8visual.com

For my Beloved

Felix, Connor & Carson

my Parents, Brother, Family & Tribe.

YOU ARE THE BEAT OF MY HEART

a *Family* is
a little world created
by *Love* ♥

**connecting**

RHONDAZARATE.COM

rhondazaratelifestyle | rhondazarate | rhondazaratelifestyle@gmail

My greatest desire is that this Planner helps you **Find Your Happy**. The path you are about to embark on is a journey to your self-discovery.

In the following pages, you will be asked questions, motivated to dream big, and encouraged to adapt yourself to new rituals & routines to enhance your life. You will be given tools that will help you create a life, tailor-made just for you. Think less and follow your heart more.

Relax, let the music of your soul whisper your true authentic song... watch how your journey plays out right before your eyes. You have been blessed with a wonderful life; Live it well, my friend, always with passion & intention.

Say yes to this juicy, delicious ride. Roll up your sleeves, take a belly-deep breath, lean into this, get centered, take swift, deliberate actions and put some skin in the game.

You truly have to believe with every fiber of your being that you deserve to be over the moon happy. Take simple actions daily to find these happy moments. They are everywhere. You just have to open your eyes and enjoy their beauty.

---

Okay, the pep talk is over! Now what? YOU might be wondering: so how do I find this happily-ever-after life? Well, my friend, I have a newsflash! It is not by crossing your fingers and toes or clicking your heels together, nor by wishing upon a star. Sorry, it's not going to happen like that. You are going to find your happy in a deliberate yet positively fabulous way.

Finding your happy is about making a plan, then working the plan. It will take consistent action to make things happen for you. Manifest with clarity exactly what it is you want with a big HELL TO THE YES! to the universe.

Through your own effort and belief deep in your core, good things are always going to happen to you, they will. Having a deep sense of gratitude, lots of guts to shake things up and the dedication to live your life by how you feel instead of what you think.

If you make this the most important guide for how you live your life, amazing things are going to happen, creating a much sweeter and richer journey.

Many hugs to you, I hope you enjoy this gift of a heartfelt journey called LIFE.

*Rhonda xoxo*

*"The biggest adventure you can ever take is to live the life of your dreams."* ~ Oprah Winfrey

# Finding Your Inner Fire and Who You Really Are

Hmmm…what lights you up? Everything! Or maybe nothing. We really can't figure it out sometimes, BUT that's okay. No worries! Let's just push forward with self-love and ponder the essential elements of our lives.

♥ **PLAN OF ACTION #1**

Grab your favorite drink (wine of choice or a hot tea) and your cherished pen, the kind which glides in your hand and makes the words look like art as they flow easily onto the paper.

Find a quiet, soothing, cozy space that you can comfortably sink into.

Take four deep, hurt-your-lung kind of breaths: the kind that sounds like Darth Vader, in through your nose and out through your mouth. Relax & enjoy!

Set a timer for 5 minutes. Write, write and write about anything and everything that comes to your mind. Whatever you feel that brings you any kind of JOY in your life!

_____

_____

_____

_____

_____

_____

_____

_____

_____

_____

_____

_____

_____

_____

# Composing Your Thoughts and Finding Your Clarity

I hope that you have a big smile on your face and you're starting to feel your **soul stirring**. Your beautiful **heart** is beginning to **sing**. Now, let's calm down and compose our thoughts. Isn't this so much fun to discover who you really are? Your true, authentic self!

♥ **PLAN OF ACTION #2**

Write the first thing that comes to your mind. Don't over-think this. Enjoy the journey of reconnecting with your soul.

What stands between you & your happy heart?_____

How do you make the world a better place and what are you most proud of?_____
_____

When was the last time you had a belly laugh? What made you laugh?_____
_____

Who are the people you truly love?_____

What are you doing for them to make them feel special?_____

From your life experiences, what lesson has life taught you?_____
_____

Is your home cluttered or organized?_____

Who can you relax with and be yourself around?_____

Do you have anything special you are looking forward to?_____

How often do you make a point of listening to your favorite music, and have you made a playlist for yourself?
_____

What did you want to be when you grew up?_____

What gift could you give to that special someone in your life?_____

What is your favorite color?_____

Name something that you could change to enhance the quality of your life?_____
_____

Who has inspired you and what wisdom did you take from them?_____
_____

How would you best describe yourself in 3 words?_____

_____

How do you celebrate the things you have in your life?_____

_____

Name three things you like to do for fun._____

When do you lose track of time? What are you doing?_____

_____

Do you ever create space for quiet & peace?_____

What is your blood type?_____

When do you feel sexy?_____

What are 3 things you love about your body?_____

Standing at the gates of heaven, a spirit asks "why do you think I should let you in?"_____

_____

Do you ever treat yourself to fresh flowers?_____

What are three yummy foods you love?_____

What is your favorite season and why?_____

What do you know for sure?_____

How do others describe who you are?_____

Do you have any kind of spiritual connection?_____

What are the five most important qualities in your life partner?_____

_____

What do you do that enhances your creativity?_____

_____

Does your body respond best to yoga/meditation, weights or cardio?_____

Are you an early bird or a night owl?_____

Have you loved deeply, holding nothing back? Describe how it felt:_____

_____

What is your favorite memory as a child and why is that?_____

_____

Your dream career. What would it be and why? You have zero limitations, just go for it!_____

_____

In this beautiful world of ours, where would you want to live, if money was not a concern?_____

_____

How do you contribute to your community?_____

What was the greatest adventure of your life?_____

What are you going to conquer this year?_____

What is your favorite place to visit?_____

What is your life's purpose?_____

What do you owe yourself?_____

What kinds of clothes do you feel more like yourself in?_____

How much money do you need a month to be happy?_____

What have you overcome that has made you stronger?_____

_____

What is the next move in your life?_____

Who could you mentor and how?_____

What advice would you give your younger self?_____

_____

Do you know how you spend your money each month? What can you do to keep better track of your finances?

_____

Who are the five most important people in your tribe?_____

_____

When was the last time you had a massage or bubble bath?_____

What cheers you up?_____

Where would you prefer to live: city, country or beach?_____

What are your specific plans for the next five years?_____

_____

_____

_____

# Fast-Forwarding Your Life, To Work Your Way Backward

Visualize this: you are on your deathbed preparing to pass from this lifetime – it's scary and sad but it's a reality that none of us can ignore. What has your journey looked like? Are you proud of the choices you have made? What would you have done the same or differently? Was your life a big, bold, beautiful experience full of joy?

Were there a few things you would have done differently? What if you had a do-over button, how many times would you have pushed it?

How would you create a life that would be perfect for you? What would put JOY in your heart and a SMILE on your face? What would make the transitional journey set out before you one without regrets or missed opportunities?

♥ **PLAN OF ACTION #3**

For a few minutes, dwell on these questions as you fast- forward and review your life at a future time. On the lines below write the story of your wonderful life's journey.

**Write whatever comes to your mind; it is your heart speaking to you. Let the questions below be a guide for you.**

Where did you choose to live? What did your home look like? Was it in the city or country? What style was it? What was the view from your front door? Were you married in your vision? How many kids/pets did you have? What did your spouse look like? What special qualities did he or she have? What was your career? How much money did you make in a month? What was your appearance? Did you follow a certain style? What kind of friends did you surround yourself with and who was in your tribe? What kind of fun activities did you engage in? Tell me about some of the most memorable places you travelled to! What are some of your fondest memories? Did you throw grand dinner parties, take chances and live large? What did you do to make a difference in the lives of others? How have you left an imprint in the world you are leaving? Did you create a life that you're proud of? Did you never miss an opportunity handed to you?

_____

_____

_____

_____

_____

_____

_____

_____

_____

_Where life begins...and love never ends:_
_Family_ ♥

# Creatively Creating My Happy Life

Now you are lit up, filled with clarity & zoomed ahead, taking a peek at your future life.

It's now time to play, create a Vision for the Life YOU WANT. It is important to see your dreams on the paper everyday. It's time for the real fun to start!

This is the time to linger and play, with the newfound gift of clarity as to what your soul is whispering to your heart. The power of Clarity is such a gift in one's life.

**Your manifestations will attract and create a magical life beyond your wildest dreams**

♥ **PLAN OF ACTION #4**

Take some time to turn on your favorite music, zen out and be free. Create any kind of collage that is beautiful to your heart. Set the intention that you want the beauty of these two pages to become the reality of your life.

Clip, paste, scribble, draw, gather magazine pictures or computer images - whatever your "Authentic Heart" desires. Relax. There are no rules around this! Enjoy the process. You deserve to play and have some fun.

# The Clarity For How I Want To Feel Daily In My Life

Now that you have remembered who you are and what you like and you have visualized what you want in your life, it is time to focus on how you want to **feel**. This is the most important aspect of your life: to live it by how you **feel** and really tap into that. Below are words that should further stir your soul to your true awakening.

Being true to your Authentic Journey is based on how you handle your emotions every single day. Below are columns of beautiful **AUTHENTIC HEART SOUL WORDS**.

♥ **PLAN OF ACTION #5**

Say each word out loud, letting all of your senses emerge as you utter it. How do you react to each word? Savor it. Feel it. If it empowers you and makes you feel like your true self is emerging, then you're on to something. When a word seems like it is part of your heart and it jumps out of the page, circle it. Explore these words for 5 minutes.

| | | | | | | | |
|---|---|---|---|---|---|---|---|
| Grounded | Healthy | Lovable | Selfless | Spiritual | Sacred | Strong | |
| Able | Leader | Stoked | Loyal | Unstoppable | Jazzed | Smart | Fearless |
| Worthy | Edgy | Exhilarated | Ageless | Family Centered | Gallant | Vortex | |
| Aligned | Content | Rooted | Radiant | Joyous | Yogi-Licious | Goddess Like | |
| Voluptuous | Evolved | Creative | Ecstatic | Gladiator | Tribally-Connected | | |
| Sweet | Soulful | Light-Hearted | Growing | Safe | Flowering | Authentic | Bold |
| Driven | Enchanting | Sharp | Supported | Pure | Open | Kick-Ass | Grateful |
| Devoted | Free | Energized | Adored | Brave | Organic | Peaceful | Seductive |
| Blissful | Kind | Giving | Adventurous | Humble | Trusting | Motivated | |
| Commander | Weightless | Feminine | Angelic | Graceful | Unpredictable | | |
| Complete | Clear | Generous | Spontaneous | Merry | Advantageous | | |
| Sparky | Truth Speaker | Connected | Invincible | Happy | Passionate | | |
| Influential | Classic | Carefree | Loved | Sexi-Licious | Enraptured | Athletic | |
| Have Game | Brilliant | Heroic | Buoyant | Funny | Playful | Audacious | Soaring |
| Lion-Hearted | Radiant | Booming | Chic | Thriving | Financially Secure | | |
| Sparkly | Fabulous | Elegant | Disciplined | Eclectic | Powerful | Ability | |

Slowly and with casual ease, choose your six chosen beloved words, the ones that make you feel so good, you can almost bust out of your skin. Place them on the six lines below. Write them beautifully; lovingly on the lines. These words are now your compass which will guide you in navigating towards creating your most AUTHENTICALLY DELICIOUS LIFE, JUST BY YOU FOR YOU.

# A PROMISE TO MYSELF MANTRA

Prioritizing your heart words in your day to day life makes you feel complete. When your feelings become your number one priority, your life will just fall into place harmoniously, each moment filled with joy and an effortless energy flow.

Place your beloved heart words on the lines below.

_____    _____    _____

_____    _____    _____

I declare from this moment on that I will live my life by how I feel.
Making my choices and taking action from a place of being centered
with clear boundaries of what I will and will not accept in my life.

I will strive to honor my **authentic heart** in all that I do.

I will keep the harmony & balance in my life, so
that I can be happy with my own truth.

I am so grateful for all of my blessings, for having this
opportunity to live my best life chosen just by me - for me.

**Making happiness my main priority.**

I declare this to be my personal truth and so it shall be.

THANK YOU. THANK YOU. THANK YOU.

# The How-To Page

Figuring out the Find Your Happy Planner System

## ♥ PLAN OF ACTION #7

Explanation of Monthly Goals, Plans, and Observations

**1** **Goals to Complete:** Always go towards your goals.

**2** **Places to Explore:** Get out in the world!

**3** **Reminders:** What to buy.

**4** **Not to Miss:** Reminders for you.

**5** **What Books are You Reading?** Books are brain food.

**6** **Plan of Action Space:** What is your plan?

**7** **What Improvements Happened in Your Life this Month?** Practice gratitude.

**8** **List Good Deeds You Shared with Others:** Remember to share the love.

**9** **What Did You do that was Fun or Spontaneous?** The importance of play!

**10** **How Did You Spoil / Treat Yourself this Month?** Remember, it's all about self-care.

**11** **Something New:** What have you tried out recently?

**12** **Manifestation Station:** What do you want to attract? Declare your intentions!

**13** **Journaling Spot:** Highlight the good times this month.

**14** **Month at a Glance:** Keep all your info at your fingertips!

## Explanation of Weekly Goals, Plans, and Observations

**1** **Write Your Six Authentic Heart Words:** From page 11. Let these words guide your life!

**2** **Your Accountability Workout Schedule:** A is for abs, C is for tracking cardio. Check when completed.

**3** **Self-care Accountability Reminder:** You are so important! Please remember to take care of yourself.

**4** **Daily Water Intake:** Record hydration it is healthy!

**5** **Wins!** Give yourself a check when you go the extra mile towards being your best you.

**6** **Happy Moments Happen Daily:** Enjoy them! Jot them down as a reminder of life's beauty.

**7** **Daily Schedule / Daily To-do List:** Keep on track with your appointments.

**8** **Daily Cash Flow:** Track your income and expenses.

**9** **Weekly Check-in:** How are you feeling?

**10** **Weekly Goal Setting Space:** What are your goals this week?

**11** **Weekly Things Not to Miss:** Reminders for you.

**12** **Projects on Your Radar**

**13** **Recipes:** Add some excitement with new recipes!

**14** **Home Decor Ideas:** Make your home cozy and an expression of your style.

**15** **Social Tracking:** Who to call, email, or message on social media.

**16** **General To-do List**

**17** **Groceries List / Necessary Purchases**

**18** **Heart Balancing Categories:** Placing a checkmark in each category makes it easier to see what your lacking areas are and where they are not. When you consistently have an empty space in one area of life, your life is not balanced. Give that area the attention it needs and your heart will sing! This is the key to having a well rounded beautiful life.

**19** **Happy Heart Moments:** Make notes on good things that have come to you this week.

**20** **Weekly One Word Exercise:** One word that describes who you are this week.

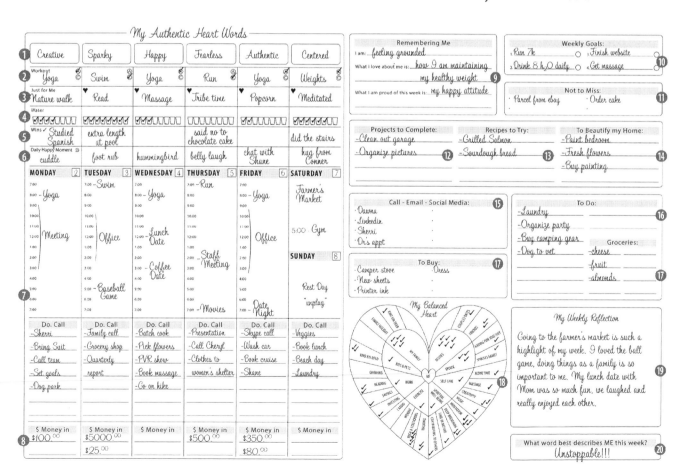

**This Month ♥**

### Goals to Complete:

1. _____ ○
2. _____ ○
3. _____ ○
4. _____ ○
5. _____ ○

### Places to Explore:

_____
_____
_____
_____
_____

### To Buy:

· · 
· · 
· · 

### Not to Miss:

· · 
· · 
· · 

### Favorite Books I am Reading:

· · 
· · 

# Month: _____

| SUNDAY | MONDAY | TUESDAY |
|---|---|---|
|  |  |  |
|  |  |  |
|  |  |  |
|  |  |  |
|  |  |  |

### ♥ PLAN OF ACTION

| Work: | Personal: | Misc: |
|---|---|---|
| ○ _____ | ○ _____ | ○ _____ |
| ○ _____ | ○ _____ | ○ _____ |
| ○ _____ | ○ _____ | ○ _____ |
| ○ _____ | ○ _____ | ○ _____ |
| ○ _____ | ○ _____ | ○ _____ |
| ○ _____ | ○ _____ | ○ _____ |
| ○ _____ | ○ _____ | ○ _____ |
| ○ _____ | ○ _____ | ○ _____ |

*"Happiness isn't about getting what you want all the time.*
*It's about loving what you have and being grateful for it."* ~ *Unknown*

| WEDNESDAY | THURSDAY | FRIDAY | SATURDAY |
|---|---|---|---|
|  |  |  |  |
|  |  |  |  |
|  |  |  |  |
|  |  |  |  |
|  |  |  |  |

## What made my ♥ happy this month...

_____
_____
_____
_____
_____
_____
_____

With gratitude & love, thank you.

## My Accomplishments this Month

### Improvements In My Life:
.
.
.
.

### Good Deeds Done:
.
.
.
.

### Fun and Spontaneous:
.
.
.
.

### I Treated Myself To:
.
.
.
.

### New Experiences:
.
.
.
.

### My Manifestation List:

| | CLAIM AS TRUE | DATE RECEIVED |
|---|---|---|
| 1. | _____ | _____ |
| 2. | _____ | _____ |
| 3. | _____ | _____ |
| 4. | _____ | _____ |
| 5. | _____ | _____ |

# $ Keeping Track of the Flow of it All

**Month:** _____

| DATES + DETAILS | MONEY IN | SAVINGS | SHARING WITH OTHERS | INSURANCE + HEALTH EXPENSES | HOUSE EXPENSES | GROCERIES | TRANSPORTATION EXPENSES | ENTERTAINMENT + FUN EXPENSES | HOLIDAY EXPENSES | PERSONAL EXPENSES | DINING OUT | MISC |
|---|---|---|---|---|---|---|---|---|---|---|---|---|
|  |  |  |  |  |  |  |  |  |  |  |  |  |
|  |  |  |  |  |  |  |  |  |  |  |  |  |
|  |  |  |  |  |  |  |  |  |  |  |  |  |
|  |  |  |  |  |  |  |  |  |  |  |  |  |
|  |  |  |  |  |  |  |  |  |  |  |  |  |
|  |  |  |  |  |  |  |  |  |  |  |  |  |
|  |  |  |  |  |  |  |  |  |  |  |  |  |
|  |  |  |  |  |  |  |  |  |  |  |  |  |
|  |  |  |  |  |  |  |  |  |  |  |  |  |
|  |  |  |  |  |  |  |  |  |  |  |  |  |
|  |  |  |  |  |  |  |  |  |  |  |  |  |
|  |  |  |  |  |  |  |  |  |  |  |  |  |
|  |  |  |  |  |  |  |  |  |  |  |  |  |
|  |  |  |  |  |  |  |  |  |  |  |  |  |
|  |  |  |  |  |  |  |  |  |  |  |  |  |
| $ TOTALS |  |  |  |  |  |  |  |  |  |  |  |  |

# My Journaling Space ♥

# My Authentic Heart Words

| | | | | | |
|---|---|---|---|---|---|
| | | | | | |

| | | | | | | |
|---|---|---|---|---|---|---|
| Workout | Ⓐ Ⓒ | Ⓐ Ⓒ | Ⓐ Ⓒ | Ⓐ Ⓒ | Ⓐ Ⓒ | Ⓐ Ⓒ |
| Just for Me | ♥ | ♥ | ♥ | ♥ | ♥ | |
| Water | ⬠⬠⬠⬠⬠⬠ | ⬠⬠⬠⬠⬠⬠ | ⬠⬠⬠⬠⬠⬠ | ⬠⬠⬠⬠⬠⬠ | ⬠⬠⬠⬠⬠⬠ | ⬠⬠⬠⬠⬠⬠ |
| Wins ✓ | | | | | | |
| Daily Happy Moment ☺ | | | | | | |

| MONDAY ☐ | TUESDAY ☐ | WEDNESDAY ☐ | THURSDAY ☐ | FRIDAY ☐ | SATURDAY ☐ |
|---|---|---|---|---|---|
| 7:00 | 7:00 | 7:00 | 7:00 | 7:00 | |
| 8:00 | 8:00 | 8:00 | 8:00 | 8:00 | |
| 9:00 | 9:00 | 9:00 | 9:00 | 9:00 | |
| 10:00 | 10:00 | 10:00 | 10:00 | 10:00 | |
| 11:00 | 11:00 | 11:00 | 11:00 | 11:00 | |
| 12:00 | 12:00 | 12:00 | 12:00 | 12:00 | |
| 1:00 | 1:00 | 1:00 | 1:00 | 1:00 | |
| 2:00 | 2:00 | 2:00 | 2:00 | 2:00 | SUNDAY ☐ |
| 3:00 | 3:00 | 3:00 | 3:00 | 3:00 | |
| 4:00 | 4:00 | 4:00 | 4:00 | 4:00 | |
| 5:00 | 5:00 | 5:00 | 5:00 | 5:00 | |
| 6:00 | 6:00 | 6:00 | 6:00 | 6:00 | |
| 7:00 | 7:00 | 7:00 | 7:00 | 7:00 | |

| Do. Call | Do. Call | Do. Call | Do. Call | Do. Call | Do. Call |
|---|---|---|---|---|---|
| | | | | | |

| $ Money in | $ Money in | $ Money in | $ Money in | $ Money in | $ Money in |
|---|---|---|---|---|---|
| | | | | | |

## Remembering Me

I am: _____

What I love about me is: _____

_____

What I am proud of this week is: _____

_____

## Weekly Goals:

1. _____ ◯   3. _____ ◯

2. _____ ◯   4. _____ ◯

## Not to Miss:

·       ·

·       ·

## Projects to Complete:

_____

_____

_____

_____

## Recipes to Try:

_____

_____

_____

_____

## To Beautify my Home:

_____

_____

_____

_____

## Call - Email - Social Media:

·       ·

·       ·

·       ·

·       ·

## To Do:

_____

_____

_____

_____

## Groceries:

_____  _____

_____  _____

_____  _____

_____  _____

## To Buy:

·       ·

·       ·

·       ·

*My Balanced Heart*

KIND KIN DEED
FAMILY HOLIDAY
COUPLES DATES
FRIENDS
HAVING FUN TOGETHER
KIND KID DEED
MY FAMILY
BESTIES
SPOUSES FAMILY
GROWING
KIDS & PETS
SPOUSE
ALONE TIME
READING
ME
SELF CARE
MASSAGE
WORK
SAVINGS
CREATIVITY
INVESTING
EXERCISE
SPIRITUAL WELL BEING
MUSIC
CARDIO
MEDITATION
WEIGHT
YOGA & STRETCHING
WALKING
DEEP BREATHING
CONTRIBUTING TO OTHERS
TIME IN NATURE

*My Weekly Reflection*

## What word best describes ME this week?

# My Authentic Heart Words

|  |  |  |  |  |  |
|---|---|---|---|---|---|
|  |  |  |  |  |  |

| Workout | Ⓐ Ⓒ | Ⓐ Ⓒ | Ⓐ Ⓒ | Ⓐ Ⓒ | Ⓐ Ⓒ | Ⓐ Ⓒ |
|---|---|---|---|---|---|---|
| Just for Me | ♥ | ♥ | ♥ | ♥ | ♥ | |
| Water | ▭▭▭▭▭▭ | ▭▭▭▭▭▭ | ▭▭▭▭▭▭ | ▭▭▭▭▭▭ | ▭▭▭▭▭▭ | ▭▭▭▭▭▭ |
| Wins ✓ | | | | | | |
| Daily Happy Moment ☺ | | | | | | |

| MONDAY ☐ | TUESDAY ☐ | WEDNESDAY ☐ | THURSDAY ☐ | FRIDAY ☐ | SATURDAY ☐ |
|---|---|---|---|---|---|
| 7:00 | 7:00 | 7:00 | 7:00 | 7:00 | |
| 8:00 | 8:00 | 8:00 | 8:00 | 8:00 | |
| 9:00 | 9:00 | 9:00 | 9:00 | 9:00 | |
| 10:00 | 10:00 | 10:00 | 10:00 | 10:00 | |
| 11:00 | 11:00 | 11:00 | 11:00 | 11:00 | |
| 12:00 | 12:00 | 12:00 | 12:00 | 12:00 | |
| 1:00 | 1:00 | 1:00 | 1:00 | 1:00 | |
| 2:00 | 2:00 | 2:00 | 2:00 | 2:00 | SUNDAY ☐ |
| 3:00 | 3:00 | 3:00 | 3:00 | 3:00 | |
| 4:00 | 4:00 | 4:00 | 4:00 | 4:00 | |
| 5:00 | 5:00 | 5:00 | 5:00 | 5:00 | |
| 6:00 | 6:00 | 6:00 | 6:00 | 6:00 | |
| 7:00 | 7:00 | 7:00 | 7:00 | 7:00 | |

| Do. Call | Do. Call | Do. Call | Do. Call | Do. Call | Do. Call |
|---|---|---|---|---|---|
| | | | | | |

| $ Money in | $ Money in | $ Money in | $ Money in | $ Money in | $ Money in |
|---|---|---|---|---|---|
| | | | | | |

## Remembering Me

I am: _____

What I love about me is: _____

_____

What I am proud of this week is: _____

_____

## Weekly Goals:

1. _____ ○   3. _____ ○

2. _____ ○   4. _____ ○

## Not to Miss:

.      .

.      .

## Projects to Complete:

_____

_____

_____

_____

## Recipes to Try:

_____

_____

_____

_____

## To Beautify my Home:

_____

_____

_____

_____

## Call - Email - Social Media:

.      .

.      .

.      .

.      .

## To Do:

_____   _____

_____   _____

_____

## Groceries:

_____   _____   _____

_____   _____   _____

## To Buy:

.      .

.      .

### My Balanced Heart

KIND KIN DEED

FAMILY HOLIDAY

COUPLES DATES

FRIENDS

HAVING FUN TOGETHER

MY FAMILY

BESTIES

SPOUSES FAMILY

KIND KID DEED

KIDS & PETS

SPOUSE

GROWING

ME

SELF CARE

ALONE TIME

READING

WORK

MASSAGE

SAVINGS

EXERCISE

SPIRITUAL WELL BEING

CREATIVITY

INVESTING

MUSIC

CARDIO

MEDITATION

WEIGHT

DEEP BREATHING

YOGA & STRETCHING

WALKING

TIME IN NATURE

CONTRIBUTING TO OTHERS

### My Weekly Reflection

## What word best describes ME this week?

# My Authentic Heart Words

| | | | | | |
|---|---|---|---|---|---|
| | | | | | |

| Workout | Ⓐ Ⓒ | Ⓐ Ⓒ | Ⓐ Ⓒ | Ⓐ Ⓒ | Ⓐ Ⓒ | Ⓐ Ⓒ |
|---|---|---|---|---|---|---|
| Just for Me | ♥ | ♥ | ♥ | ♥ | ♥ | |
| Water | ⊔⊔⊔⊔⊔⊔ | ⊔⊔⊔⊔⊔⊔ | ⊔⊔⊔⊔⊔⊔ | ⊔⊔⊔⊔⊔⊔ | ⊔⊔⊔⊔⊔⊔ | ⊔⊔⊔⊔⊔⊔ |
| Wins ✓ | | | | | | |
| Daily Happy Moment ☺ | | | | | | |

| MONDAY ☐ | TUESDAY ☐ | WEDNESDAY ☐ | THURSDAY ☐ | FRIDAY ☐ | SATURDAY ☐ |
|---|---|---|---|---|---|
| 7:00 | 7:00 | 7:00 | 7:00 | 7:00 | |
| 8:00 | 8:00 | 8:00 | 8:00 | 8:00 | |
| 9:00 | 9:00 | 9:00 | 9:00 | 9:00 | |
| 10:00 | 10:00 | 10:00 | 10:00 | 10:00 | |
| 11:00 | 11:00 | 11:00 | 11:00 | 11:00 | |
| 12:00 | 12:00 | 12:00 | 12:00 | 12:00 | |
| 1:00 | 1:00 | 1:00 | 1:00 | 1:00 | |
| 2:00 | 2:00 | 2:00 | 2:00 | 2:00 | SUNDAY ☐ |
| 3:00 | 3:00 | 3:00 | 3:00 | 3:00 | |
| 4:00 | 4:00 | 4:00 | 4:00 | 4:00 | |
| 5:00 | 5:00 | 5:00 | 5:00 | 5:00 | |
| 6:00 | 6:00 | 6:00 | 6:00 | 6:00 | |
| 7:00 | 7:00 | 7:00 | 7:00 | 7:00 | |

| Do. Call | Do. Call | Do. Call | Do. Call | Do. Call | Do. Call |
|---|---|---|---|---|---|
| | | | | | |

| $ Money in | $ Money in | $ Money in | $ Money in | $ Money in | $ Money in |
|---|---|---|---|---|---|
| | | | | | |

## Remembering Me

I am: _____

What I love about me is: _____

_____

What I am proud of this week is: _____

_____

## Weekly Goals:

1. _____ ◯   3. _____ ◯

2. _____ ◯   4. _____ ◯

## Not to Miss:

· _____   · _____

· _____   · _____

## Projects to Complete:

_____
_____
_____
_____

## Recipes to Try:

_____
_____
_____
_____

## To Beautify my Home:

_____
_____
_____
_____

## Call - Email - Social Media:

· _____   · _____
· _____   · _____
· _____   · _____
· _____   · _____

## To Buy:

· _____   · _____
· _____   · _____

## To Do:

_____  _____
_____  _____
_____

### Groceries:

_____  _____  _____
_____  _____  _____
_____  _____  _____

## My Balanced Heart

KIND KIN DEED
FAMILY HOLIDAY
COUPLES DATES
FRIENDS
HAVING FUN TOGETHER
KIND KID DEED
MY FAMILY
BESTIES
SPOUSES FAMILY
GROWING
KIDS & PETS
SPOUSE
ALONE TIME
READING
ME
SELF CARE
MASSAGE
WORK
SAVINGS
CREATIVITY
INVESTING
EXERCISE
SPIRITUAL WELL BEING
MUSIC
CARDIO
MEDITATION
WEIGHT
YOGA & STRETCHING
WALKING
TIME IN NATURE
DEEP BREATHING
CONTRIBUTING TO OTHERS

## My Weekly Reflection

## What word best describes ME this week?

23

# My Authentic Heart Words

|  |  |  |  |  |  |
|---|---|---|---|---|---|
| | | | | | |

| | | | | | | |
|---|---|---|---|---|---|---|
| Workout | Ⓐ Ⓒ | Ⓐ Ⓒ | Ⓐ Ⓒ | Ⓐ Ⓒ | Ⓐ Ⓒ | Ⓐ Ⓒ |
| Just for Me | ♥ | ♥ | ♥ | ♥ | ♥ | |
| Water | ⊔⊔⊔⊔⊔⊔ | ⊔⊔⊔⊔⊔⊔ | ⊔⊔⊔⊔⊔⊔ | ⊔⊔⊔⊔⊔⊔ | ⊔⊔⊔⊔⊔⊔ | ⊔⊔⊔⊔⊔⊔ |
| Wins ✓ | | | | | | |
| Daily Happy Moment ☺ | | | | | | |

| MONDAY ☐ | TUESDAY ☐ | WEDNESDAY ☐ | THURSDAY ☐ | FRIDAY ☐ | SATURDAY ☐ |
|---|---|---|---|---|---|
| 7:00 | 7:00 | 7:00 | 7:00 | 7:00 | |
| 8:00 | 8:00 | 8:00 | 8:00 | 8:00 | |
| 9:00 | 9:00 | 9:00 | 9:00 | 9:00 | |
| 10:00 | 10:00 | 10:00 | 10:00 | 10:00 | |
| 11:00 | 11:00 | 11:00 | 11:00 | 11:00 | |
| 12:00 | 12:00 | 12:00 | 12:00 | 12:00 | |
| 1:00 | 1:00 | 1:00 | 1:00 | 1:00 | |
| 2:00 | 2:00 | 2:00 | 2:00 | 2:00 | SUNDAY ☐ |
| 3:00 | 3:00 | 3:00 | 3:00 | 3:00 | |
| 4:00 | 4:00 | 4:00 | 4:00 | 4:00 | |
| 5:00 | 5:00 | 5:00 | 5:00 | 5:00 | |
| 6:00 | 6:00 | 6:00 | 6:00 | 6:00 | |
| 7:00 | 7:00 | 7:00 | 7:00 | 7:00 | |

| Do. Call | Do. Call | Do. Call | Do. Call | Do. Call | Do. Call |
|---|---|---|---|---|---|
| | | | | | |

| $ Money in | $ Money in | $ Money in | $ Money in | $ Money in | $ Money in |
|---|---|---|---|---|---|
| | | | | | |

## Remembering Me

I am: _____

What I love about me is: _____

_____

What I am proud of this week is: _____

_____

## Weekly Goals:

1. _____ ○   3. _____ ○

2. _____ ○   4. _____ ○

## Not to Miss:

· _____     · _____

· _____     · _____

## Projects to Complete:

_____

_____

_____

_____

## Recipes to Try:

_____

_____

_____

_____

## To Beautify my Home:

_____

_____

_____

_____

## Call - Email - Social Media:

· _____     · _____

· _____     · _____

· _____     · _____

· _____     · _____

## To Buy:

· _____     · _____

· _____     · _____

## To Do:

_____     _____

_____     _____

_____     

## Groceries:

_____     _____   _____

_____     _____   _____

_____     _____   _____

_____     _____   _____

### My Balanced Heart

FAMILY HOLIDAY, KIND KIN DEED, COUPLES DATES, FRIENDS, HAVING FUN TOGETHER, KIND KID DEED, MY FAMILY, BESTIES, SPOUSES FAMILY, GROWING, KIDS & PETS, SPOUSE, ALONE TIME, READING, WORK, ME, SELF CARE, MASSAGE, SAVINGS, EXERCISE, SPIRITUAL WELL BEING, CREATIVITY, INVESTING, CARDIO, MUSIC, WEIGHT, YOGA & STRETCHING, WALKING, CONTRIBUTING TO OTHERS, TIME IN NATURE, DEEP BREATHING, MEDITATION

### My Weekly Reflection

## What word best describes ME this week?

| | | | | | |
|---|---|---|---|---|---|

| Workout | Ⓐ Ⓒ | Ⓐ Ⓒ | Ⓐ Ⓒ | Ⓐ Ⓒ | Ⓐ Ⓒ | Ⓐ Ⓒ |
|---|---|---|---|---|---|---|
| Just for Me | ♥ | ♥ | ♥ | ♥ | ♥ | |
| Water | ⊔⊔⊔⊔⊔⊔ | ⊔⊔⊔⊔⊔⊔ | ⊔⊔⊔⊔⊔⊔ | ⊔⊔⊔⊔⊔⊔ | ⊔⊔⊔⊔⊔⊔ | ⊔⊔⊔⊔⊔⊔ |
| Wins ✓ | | | | | | |
| Daily Happy Moment ☺ | | | | | | |

| MONDAY ☐ | TUESDAY ☐ | WEDNESDAY ☐ | THURSDAY ☐ | FRIDAY ☐ | SATURDAY ☐ |
|---|---|---|---|---|---|
| 7:00 | 7:00 | 7:00 | 7:00 | 7:00 | |
| 8:00 | 8:00 | 8:00 | 8:00 | 8:00 | |
| 9:00 | 9:00 | 9:00 | 9:00 | 9:00 | |
| 10:00 | 10:00 | 10:00 | 10:00 | 10:00 | |
| 11:00 | 11:00 | 11:00 | 11:00 | 11:00 | |
| 12:00 | 12:00 | 12:00 | 12:00 | 12:00 | |
| 1:00 | 1:00 | 1:00 | 1:00 | 1:00 | |
| 2:00 | 2:00 | 2:00 | 2:00 | 2:00 | SUNDAY ☐ |
| 3:00 | 3:00 | 3:00 | 3:00 | 3:00 | |
| 4:00 | 4:00 | 4:00 | 4:00 | 4:00 | |
| 5:00 | 5:00 | 5:00 | 5:00 | 5:00 | |
| 6:00 | 6:00 | 6:00 | 6:00 | 6:00 | |
| 7:00 | 7:00 | 7:00 | 7:00 | 7:00 | |

| Do. Call | Do. Call | Do. Call | Do. Call | Do. Call | Do. Call |
|---|---|---|---|---|---|

| $ Money in | $ Money in | $ Money in | $ Money in | $ Money in | $ Money in |
|---|---|---|---|---|---|

## Remembering Me

I am: _____

What I love about me is: _____

_____

What I am proud of this week is: _____

_____

## Weekly Goals:

1. _____ ○   3. _____ ○

2. _____ ○   4. _____ ○

## Not to Miss:

· 

· 

· 

· 

## Projects to Complete:

_____
_____
_____
_____

## Recipes to Try:

_____
_____
_____
_____

## To Beautify my Home:

_____
_____
_____
_____

## Call - Email - Social Media:

· 

· 

· 

· 

· 

· 

· 

· 

## To Do:

_____
_____
_____
_____

## Groceries:

_____   _____
_____   _____
_____   _____

## To Buy:

· 

· 

· 

· 

· 

· 

### My Balanced Heart

FAMILY HOLIDAY
KIND KIN DEED
COUPLES DATES
FRIENDS
HAVING FUN TOGETHER
KIND KID DEED
MY FAMILY
BESTIES
SPOUSES FAMILY
GROWING
KIDS & PETS
SPOUSE
ALONE TIME
READING
WORK
ME
SELF CARE
MASSAGE
SAVINGS
EXERCISE
SPIRITUAL WELL BEING
CREATIVITY
INVESTING
MUSIC
CARDIO
MEDITATION
WEIGHT
DEEP BREATHING
YOGA & STRETCHING
WALKING
CONTRIBUTING TO OTHERS
TIME IN NATURE

### My Weekly Reflection

### What word best describes ME this week?

## This Month ♥

### Goals to Complete:

1. _____ ○
2. _____ ○
3. _____ ○
4. _____ ○
5. _____ ○

### Places to Explore:

_____
_____
_____
_____
_____

### To Buy:

· _____    · _____
· _____    · _____
· _____    · _____

### Not to Miss:

· _____    · _____
· _____    · _____
· _____    · _____

### Favorite Books I am Reading:

· _____    · _____
· _____    · _____

# Month: _____

| SUNDAY | MONDAY | TUESDAY |
|--------|--------|---------|
|        |        |         |
|        |        |         |
|        |        |         |
|        |        |         |
|        |        |         |

### ♥ PLAN OF ACTION

| Work: | Personal: | Misc: |
|-------|-----------|-------|
| ○ _____ | ○ _____ | ○ _____ |
| ○ _____ | ○ _____ | ○ _____ |
| ○ _____ | ○ _____ | ○ _____ |
| ○ _____ | ○ _____ | ○ _____ |
| ○ _____ | ○ _____ | ○ _____ |
| ○ _____ | ○ _____ | ○ _____ |
| ○ _____ | ○ _____ | ○ _____ |
| ○ _____ | ○ _____ | ○ _____ |

*"The only thing that will make you happy is being happy with who you are, and not who people think you are."* ~ Goldie Hawn

| WEDNESDAY | THURSDAY | FRIDAY | SATURDAY |
|---|---|---|---|
| | | | |
| | | | |
| | | | |
| | | | |
| | | | |

## What made my ♥ happy this month...

_____
_____
_____
_____
_____
_____
_____

With gratitude & love, thank you.

## My Accomplishments this Month

### Improvements In My Life:
.
.
.
.

### Good Deeds Done:
.
.
.
.

### Fun and Spontaneous:
.
.
.
.

### I Treated Myself To:
.
.
.
.

### New Experiences:
.
.
.
.

### My Manifestation List:

| | CLAIM AS TRUE | DATE RECEIVED |
|---|---|---|
| 1. | _____ | _____ |
| 2. | _____ | _____ |
| 3. | _____ | _____ |
| 4. | _____ | _____ |
| 5. | _____ | _____ |

# $ Keeping Track of the Flow of it All

**Month:** _____

| DATES + DETAILS | MONEY IN | SAVINGS | SHARING WITH OTHERS | INSURANCE + HEALTH EXPENSES | HOUSE EXPENSES | GROCERIES | TRANSPORTATION EXPENSES | ENTERTAINMENT + FUN EXPENSES | HOLIDAY EXPENSES | PERSONAL EXPENSES | DINING OUT | MISC |
|---|---|---|---|---|---|---|---|---|---|---|---|---|
| | | | | | | | | | | | | |
| | | | | | | | | | | | | |
| | | | | | | | | | | | | |
| | | | | | | | | | | | | |
| | | | | | | | | | | | | |
| | | | | | | | | | | | | |
| | | | | | | | | | | | | |
| | | | | | | | | | | | | |
| | | | | | | | | | | | | |
| | | | | | | | | | | | | |
| | | | | | | | | | | | | |
| | | | | | | | | | | | | |
| | | | | | | | | | | | | |
| | | | | | | | | | | | | |
| | | | | | | | | | | | | |
| | | | | | | | | | | | | |
| $ TOTALS | | | | | | | | | | | | |

# My Journaling Space ♥

# My Authentic Heart Words

|  |  |  |  |  |  |
|---|---|---|---|---|---|
|  |  |  |  |  |  |

| Workout | Ⓐ Ⓒ | Ⓐ Ⓒ | Ⓐ Ⓒ | Ⓐ Ⓒ | Ⓐ Ⓒ | Ⓐ Ⓒ |

| Just for Me | ♥ | ♥ | ♥ | ♥ | ♥ | |

Water

Wins ✓

Daily Happy Moment ☺

| **MONDAY** ☐ | **TUESDAY** ☐ | **WEDNESDAY** ☐ | **THURSDAY** ☐ | **FRIDAY** ☐ | **SATURDAY** ☐ |
|---|---|---|---|---|---|
| 7:00 | 7:00 | 7:00 | 7:00 | 7:00 | |
| 8:00 | 8:00 | 8:00 | 8:00 | 8:00 | |
| 9:00 | 9:00 | 9:00 | 9:00 | 9:00 | |
| 10:00 | 10:00 | 10:00 | 10:00 | 10:00 | |
| 11:00 | 11:00 | 11:00 | 11:00 | 11:00 | |
| 12:00 | 12:00 | 12:00 | 12:00 | 12:00 | |
| 1:00 | 1:00 | 1:00 | 1:00 | 1:00 | |
| 2:00 | 2:00 | 2:00 | 2:00 | 2:00 | **SUNDAY** ☐ |
| 3:00 | 3:00 | 3:00 | 3:00 | 3:00 | |
| 4:00 | 4:00 | 4:00 | 4:00 | 4:00 | |
| 5:00 | 5:00 | 5:00 | 5:00 | 5:00 | |
| 6:00 | 6:00 | 6:00 | 6:00 | 6:00 | |
| 7:00 | 7:00 | 7:00 | 7:00 | 7:00 | |

| Do. Call | Do. Call | Do. Call | Do. Call | Do. Call | Do. Call |
|---|---|---|---|---|---|
| | | | | | |

| $ Money in | $ Money in | $ Money in | $ Money in | $ Money in | $ Money in |
|---|---|---|---|---|---|
| | | | | | |

## Remembering Me

I am: _____

What I love about me is: _____

_____

What I am proud of this week is: _____

_____

## Weekly Goals:

1. _____ ○   3. _____ ○

2. _____ ○   4. _____ ○

## Not to Miss:

·       ·

·       ·

## Projects to Complete:

_____
_____
_____
_____

## Recipes to Try:

_____
_____
_____

## To Beautify my Home:

_____
_____
_____

## Call - Email - Social Media:

·       ·
·       ·
·       ·
·       ·

## To Do:

_____  _____
_____  _____
_____

## Groceries:

_____  _____ _____
_____  _____ _____
_____  _____ _____

## To Buy:

·       ·
·       ·
·       ·

### My Balanced Heart

KIND KIN DEED
FAMILY HOLIDAY
COUPLES DATES
FRIENDS
HAVING FUN TOGETHER
KIND KID DEED
MY FAMILY
BESTIES
SPOUSES FAMILY
KIDS & PETS
SPOUSE
GROWING
ME
SELF CARE
ALONE TIME
READING
WORK
MASSAGE
SAVINGS
EXERCISE
SPIRITUAL WELL BEING
CREATIVITY
INVESTING
MUSIC
CARDIO
WEIGHT
MEDITATION
YOGA & STRETCHING
WALKING
DEEP BREATHING
TIME IN NATURE
CONTRIBUTING TO OTHERS

### My Weekly Reflection

### What word best describes ME this week?

| | | | | | |
|---|---|---|---|---|---|
| | | | | | |

| | | | | | | |
|---|---|---|---|---|---|---|
| Workout | Ⓐ Ⓒ | Ⓐ Ⓒ | Ⓐ Ⓒ | Ⓐ Ⓒ | Ⓐ Ⓒ | Ⓐ Ⓒ |
| Just for Me | ♥ | ♥ | ♥ | ♥ | ♥ | |
| Water | ⊔⊔⊔⊔⊔⊔ | ⊔⊔⊔⊔⊔⊔ | ⊔⊔⊔⊔⊔⊔ | ⊔⊔⊔⊔⊔⊔ | ⊔⊔⊔⊔⊔⊔ | ⊔⊔⊔⊔⊔⊔ |
| Wins ✓ | | | | | | |
| Daily Happy Moment ☺ | | | | | | |

| MONDAY ☐ | TUESDAY ☐ | WEDNESDAY ☐ | THURSDAY ☐ | FRIDAY ☐ | SATURDAY ☐ |
|---|---|---|---|---|---|
| 7:00 | 7:00 | 7:00 | 7:00 | 7:00 | |
| 8:00 | 8:00 | 8:00 | 8:00 | 8:00 | |
| 9:00 | 9:00 | 9:00 | 9:00 | 9:00 | |
| 10:00 | 10:00 | 10:00 | 10:00 | 10:00 | |
| 11:00 | 11:00 | 11:00 | 11:00 | 11:00 | |
| 12:00 | 12:00 | 12:00 | 12:00 | 12:00 | |
| 1:00 | 1:00 | 1:00 | 1:00 | 1:00 | |
| 2:00 | 2:00 | 2:00 | 2:00 | 2:00 | SUNDAY ☐ |
| 3:00 | 3:00 | 3:00 | 3:00 | 3:00 | |
| 4:00 | 4:00 | 4:00 | 4:00 | 4:00 | |
| 5:00 | 5:00 | 5:00 | 5:00 | 5:00 | |
| 6:00 | 6:00 | 6:00 | 6:00 | 6:00 | |
| 7:00 | 7:00 | 7:00 | 7:00 | 7:00 | |

| Do. Call | Do. Call | Do. Call | Do. Call | Do. Call | Do. Call |
|---|---|---|---|---|---|
| | | | | | |

| $ Money in | $ Money in | $ Money in | $ Money in | $ Money in | $ Money in |
|---|---|---|---|---|---|
| | | | | | |

## Remembering Me

I am: _____

What I love about me is: _____

_____

What I am proud of this week is: _____

_____

## Weekly Goals:

1. _____ ◯  3. _____ ◯

2. _____ ◯  4. _____ ◯

## Not to Miss:

· _____ · _____

· _____ · _____

## Projects to Complete:

_____

_____

_____

_____

## Recipes to Try:

_____

_____

_____

## To Beautify my Home:

_____

_____

_____

## Call - Email - Social Media:

· _____ · _____

· _____ · _____

· _____ · _____

· _____ · _____

## To Buy:

· _____ · _____

· _____ · _____

· _____ · _____

## To Do:

_____ _____

_____ _____

_____ 

### Groceries:

_____ _____ _____

_____ _____ _____

_____ _____ _____

_____ _____ _____

_____ _____ _____

### My Balanced Heart

My Weekly Reflection

What word best describes ME this week?

# My Authentic Heart Words

|  |  |  |  |  |  |
|---|---|---|---|---|---|
|  |  |  |  |  |  |

| Workout | Ⓐ Ⓒ | Ⓐ Ⓒ | Ⓐ Ⓒ | Ⓐ Ⓒ | Ⓐ Ⓒ | Ⓐ Ⓒ |
|---|---|---|---|---|---|---|
| Just for Me | ♥ | ♥ | ♥ | ♥ | ♥ | |
| Water | ▢▢▢▢▢▢▢ | ▢▢▢▢▢▢▢ | ▢▢▢▢▢▢▢ | ▢▢▢▢▢▢▢ | ▢▢▢▢▢▢▢ | ▢▢▢▢▢▢▢ |
| Wins ✓ | | | | | | |
| Daily Happy Moment ☺ | | | | | | |

| MONDAY ☐ | TUESDAY ☐ | WEDNESDAY ☐ | THURSDAY ☐ | FRIDAY ☐ | SATURDAY ☐ |
|---|---|---|---|---|---|
| 7:00 | 7:00 | 7:00 | 7:00 | 7:00 | |
| 8:00 | 8:00 | 8:00 | 8:00 | 8:00 | |
| 9:00 | 9:00 | 9:00 | 9:00 | 9:00 | |
| 10:00 | 10:00 | 10:00 | 10:00 | 10:00 | |
| 11:00 | 11:00 | 11:00 | 11:00 | 11:00 | |
| 12:00 | 12:00 | 12:00 | 12:00 | 12:00 | |
| 1:00 | 1:00 | 1:00 | 1:00 | 1:00 | |
| 2:00 | 2:00 | 2:00 | 2:00 | 2:00 | SUNDAY ☐ |
| 3:00 | 3:00 | 3:00 | 3:00 | 3:00 | |
| 4:00 | 4:00 | 4:00 | 4:00 | 4:00 | |
| 5:00 | 5:00 | 5:00 | 5:00 | 5:00 | |
| 6:00 | 6:00 | 6:00 | 6:00 | 6:00 | |
| 7:00 | 7:00 | 7:00 | 7:00 | 7:00 | |

| Do. Call | Do. Call | Do. Call | Do. Call | Do. Call | Do. Call |
|---|---|---|---|---|---|
| | | | | | |

| $ Money in | $ Money in | $ Money in | $ Money in | $ Money in | $ Money in |
|---|---|---|---|---|---|
| | | | | | |

## Remembering Me

I am: _____

What I love about me is: _____

_____

What I am proud of this week is: _____

_____

## Weekly Goals:

1. _____ ◯  3. _____ ◯

2. _____ ◯  4. _____ ◯

## Not to Miss:

· _____  · _____

· _____  · _____

## Projects to Complete:

_____
_____
_____
_____

## Recipes to Try:

_____
_____
_____
_____

## To Beautify my Home:

_____
_____
_____
_____

## Call - Email - Social Media:

· _____  · _____

· _____  · _____

· _____  · _____

· _____  · _____

## To Do:

_____  _____

_____  _____

_____  ## Groceries:

_____  _____  _____

_____  _____  _____

_____  _____  _____

## To Buy:

· _____  · _____

· _____  · _____

· _____  · _____

My Balanced Heart

FAMILY HOLIDAY · KIND KIN DEED · COUPLES DATES · FRIENDS · HAVING FUN TOGETHER · KIND KID DEED · MY FAMILY · BESTIES · SPOUSES FAMILY · GROWING · KIDS & PETS · SPOUSE · ALONE TIME · READING · WORK · ME · SELF CARE · MASSAGE · SAVINGS · EXERCISE · SPIRITUAL WELL BEING · CREATIVITY · INVESTING · MUSIC · CARDIO · MEDITATION · WEIGHT · DEEP BREATHING · YOGA & STRETCHING · WALKING · TIME IN NATURE · CONTRIBUTING TO OTHERS

## My Weekly Reflection

## What word best describes ME this week?

| | | | | | |
|---|---|---|---|---|---|
| | | | | | |

| | | | | | | |
|---|---|---|---|---|---|---|
| Workout | Ⓐ Ⓒ | Ⓐ Ⓒ | Ⓐ Ⓒ | Ⓐ Ⓒ | Ⓐ Ⓒ | Ⓐ Ⓒ |
| Just for Me | ♥ | ♥ | ♥ | ♥ | ♥ | |
| Water | ▭▭▭▭▭▭ | ▭▭▭▭▭▭ | ▭▭▭▭▭▭ | ▭▭▭▭▭▭ | ▭▭▭▭▭▭ | ▭▭▭▭▭▭ |
| Wins ✓ | | | | | | |
| Daily Happy Moment ☺ | | | | | | |

| MONDAY ☐ | TUESDAY ☐ | WEDNESDAY ☐ | THURSDAY ☐ | FRIDAY ☐ | SATURDAY ☐ |
|---|---|---|---|---|---|
| 7:00 | 7:00 | 7:00 | 7:00 | 7:00 | |
| 8:00 | 8:00 | 8:00 | 8:00 | 8:00 | |
| 9:00 | 9:00 | 9:00 | 9:00 | 9:00 | |
| 10:00 | 10:00 | 10:00 | 10:00 | 10:00 | |
| 11:00 | 11:00 | 11:00 | 11:00 | 11:00 | |
| 12:00 | 12:00 | 12:00 | 12:00 | 12:00 | |
| 1:00 | 1:00 | 1:00 | 1:00 | 1:00 | |
| 2:00 | 2:00 | 2:00 | 2:00 | 2:00 | SUNDAY ☐ |
| 3:00 | 3:00 | 3:00 | 3:00 | 3:00 | |
| 4:00 | 4:00 | 4:00 | 4:00 | 4:00 | |
| 5:00 | 5:00 | 5:00 | 5:00 | 5:00 | |
| 6:00 | 6:00 | 6:00 | 6:00 | 6:00 | |
| 7:00 | 7:00 | 7:00 | 7:00 | 7:00 | |

| Do. Call | Do. Call | Do. Call | Do. Call | Do. Call | Do. Call |
|---|---|---|---|---|---|
| | | | | | |

| $ Money in | $ Money in | $ Money in | $ Money in | $ Money in | $ Money in |
|---|---|---|---|---|---|
| | | | | | |

## Remembering Me

I am: _____

What I love about me is: _____

_____

What I am proud of this week is: _____

_____

## Weekly Goals:

1. _____ ○   3. _____ ○

2. _____ ○   4. _____ ○

## Not to Miss:

·                          ·

·                          ·

## Projects to Complete:

_____

_____

_____

_____

## Recipes to Try:

_____

_____

_____

_____

## To Beautify my Home:

_____

_____

_____

_____

## Call - Email - Social Media:

·                          ·

·                          ·

·                          ·

·                          ·

## To Do:

_____

_____

_____

_____

_____

## Groceries:

_____  _____

_____  _____

_____  _____

## To Buy:

·                          ·

·                          ·

·                          ·

## My Balanced Heart

## My Weekly Reflection

What word best describes ME this week?

# My Authentic Heart Words

| | | | | | |
|---|---|---|---|---|---|
| | | | | | |

| Workout | Ⓐ Ⓒ | Ⓐ Ⓒ | Ⓐ Ⓒ | Ⓐ Ⓒ | Ⓐ Ⓒ | Ⓐ Ⓒ |
|---|---|---|---|---|---|---|
| Just for Me | ♥ | ♥ | ♥ | ♥ | ♥ | |
| Water | ▽▽▽▽▽▽▽ | ▽▽▽▽▽▽▽ | ▽▽▽▽▽▽▽ | ▽▽▽▽▽▽▽ | ▽▽▽▽▽▽▽ | ▽▽▽▽▽▽▽ |
| Wins ✓ | | | | | | |
| Daily Happy Moment ☺ | | | | | | |

| **MONDAY** ☐ | **TUESDAY** ☐ | **WEDNESDAY** ☐ | **THURSDAY** ☐ | **FRIDAY** ☐ | **SATURDAY** ☐ |
|---|---|---|---|---|---|
| 7:00 | 7:00 | 7:00 | 7:00 | 7:00 | |
| 8:00 | 8:00 | 8:00 | 8:00 | 8:00 | |
| 9:00 | 9:00 | 9:00 | 9:00 | 9:00 | |
| 10:00 | 10:00 | 10:00 | 10:00 | 10:00 | |
| 11:00 | 11:00 | 11:00 | 11:00 | 11:00 | |
| 12:00 | 12:00 | 12:00 | 12:00 | 12:00 | |
| 1:00 | 1:00 | 1:00 | 1:00 | 1:00 | |
| 2:00 | 2:00 | 2:00 | 2:00 | 2:00 | **SUNDAY** ☐ |
| 3:00 | 3:00 | 3:00 | 3:00 | 3:00 | |
| 4:00 | 4:00 | 4:00 | 4:00 | 4:00 | |
| 5:00 | 5:00 | 5:00 | 5:00 | 5:00 | |
| 6:00 | 6:00 | 6:00 | 6:00 | 6:00 | |
| 7:00 | 7:00 | 7:00 | 7:00 | 7:00 | |

| Do. Call | Do. Call | Do. Call | Do. Call | Do. Call | Do. Call |
|---|---|---|---|---|---|
| | | | | | |
| | | | | | |
| | | | | | |
| | | | | | |
| | | | | | |
| | | | | | |
| | | | | | |
| | | | | | |
| $ Money in | $ Money in | $ Money in | $ Money in | $ Money in | $ Money in |

## Remembering Me

I am: _____

What I love about me is: _____

_____

What I am proud of this week is: _____

_____

## Weekly Goals:

1. _____ ○   3. _____ ○

2. _____ ○   4. _____ ○

## Not to Miss:

·                    ·

·                    ·

## Projects to Complete:

_____

_____

_____

_____

## Recipes to Try:

_____

_____

_____

_____

## To Beautify my Home:

_____

_____

_____

_____

## Call - Email - Social Media:

·                    ·

·                    ·

·                    ·

·                    ·

## To Do:

_____   _____

_____   _____

_____

_____   ## Groceries:

_____   _____ _____

## To Buy:           _____ _____

·                    ·          _____ _____

·                    ·          _____ _____

·                    ·

### My Balanced Heart

KIND KIN DEED · FAMILY HOLIDAY · COUPLES DATES · FRIENDS · HAVING FUN TOGETHER · KIND KID DEED · MY FAMILY · BESTIES · SPOUSES FAMILY · KIDS & PETS · SPOUSE · GROWING · ME · ALONE TIME · READING · WORK · SELF CARE · MASSAGE · SAVINGS · EXERCISE · SPIRITUAL WELL BEING · CREATIVITY · INVESTING · MUSIC · CARDIO · MEDITATION · WEIGHT · YOGA & STRETCHING · WALKING · CONTRIBUTING TO OTHERS · TIME IN NATURE · DEEP BREATHING

### My Weekly Reflection

### What word best describes ME this week?

41

## This Month ♥

### Goals to Complete:

1. _____ ○
2. _____ ○
3. _____ ○
4. _____ ○
5. _____ ○

### Places to Explore:

_____

_____

_____

_____

_____

### To Buy:

·     ·

·     ·

·     ·

### Not to Miss:

·     ·

·     ·

·     ·

### Favorite Books I am Reading:

·     ·

·     ·

# Month: _____

| SUNDAY | MONDAY | TUESDAY |
|---|---|---|
|  |  |  |
|  |  |  |
|  |  |  |
|  |  |  |
|  |  |  |

## ♥ PLAN OF ACTION

| Work: | Personal: | Misc: |
|---|---|---|
| ○ _____ | ○ _____ | ○ _____ |
| ○ _____ | ○ _____ | ○ _____ |
| ○ _____ | ○ _____ | ○ _____ |
| ○ _____ | ○ _____ | ○ _____ |
| ○ _____ | ○ _____ | ○ _____ |
| ○ _____ | ○ _____ | ○ _____ |
| ○ _____ | ○ _____ | ○ _____ |
| ○ _____ | ○ _____ | ○ _____ |

*"Every accomplishment starts with the decision to try." ~ Unknown*

**My Accomplishments this Month**

| WEDNESDAY | THURSDAY | FRIDAY | SATURDAY |
|---|---|---|---|
| | | | |
| | | | |
| | | | |
| | | | |
| | | | |

Improvements In My Life:
.
.
.
.

Good Deeds Done:
.
.
.
.

Fun and Spontaneous:
.
.
.

I Treated Myself To:
.
.
.
.

New Experiences:
.
.
.
.

### What made my ♥ happy this month...

_____
_____
_____
_____
_____
_____

With gratitude & love, thank you.

My Manifestation List:

| | CLAIM AS TRUE | DATE RECEIVED |
|---|---|---|
| 1. | _____ | _____ |
| 2. | _____ | _____ |
| 3. | _____ | _____ |
| 4. | _____ | _____ |
| 5. | _____ | _____ |

# $ Keeping Track of the Flow of it All

**Month:** _____

| DATES + DETAILS | MONEY IN | SAVINGS | SHARING WITH OTHERS | INSURANCE + HEALTH EXPENSES | HOUSE EXPENSES | GROCERIES | TRANSPORTATION EXPENSES | ENTERTAINMENT + FUN EXPENSES | HOLIDAY EXPENSES | PERSONAL EXPENSES | DINING OUT | MISC |
|---|---|---|---|---|---|---|---|---|---|---|---|---|
| | | | | | | | | | | | | |
| | | | | | | | | | | | | |
| | | | | | | | | | | | | |
| | | | | | | | | | | | | |
| | | | | | | | | | | | | |
| | | | | | | | | | | | | |
| | | | | | | | | | | | | |
| | | | | | | | | | | | | |
| | | | | | | | | | | | | |
| | | | | | | | | | | | | |
| | | | | | | | | | | | | |
| | | | | | | | | | | | | |
| | | | | | | | | | | | | |
| | | | | | | | | | | | | |
| $ TOTALS | | | | | | | | | | | | |

## My Journaling Space ♥

# My Authentic Heart Words

|  |  |  |  |  |  |
|---|---|---|---|---|---|
|  |  |  |  |  |  |

| Workout | Ⓐ Ⓒ | Ⓐ Ⓒ | Ⓐ Ⓒ | Ⓐ Ⓒ | Ⓐ Ⓒ | Ⓐ Ⓒ |
|---|---|---|---|---|---|---|
| Just for Me | ♥ | ♥ | ♥ | ♥ | ♥ | |
| Water | 🥛🥛🥛🥛🥛🥛 | 🥛🥛🥛🥛🥛🥛 | 🥛🥛🥛🥛🥛🥛 | 🥛🥛🥛🥛🥛🥛 | 🥛🥛🥛🥛🥛🥛 | 🥛🥛🥛🥛🥛🥛 |
| Wins ✓ | | | | | | |
| Daily Happy Moment ☺ | | | | | | |

| MONDAY ☐ | TUESDAY ☐ | WEDNESDAY ☐ | THURSDAY ☐ | FRIDAY ☐ | SATURDAY ☐ |
|---|---|---|---|---|---|
| 7:00 | 7:00 | 7:00 | 7:00 | 7:00 | |
| 8:00 | 8:00 | 8:00 | 8:00 | 8:00 | |
| 9:00 | 9:00 | 9:00 | 9:00 | 9:00 | |
| 10:00 | 10:00 | 10:00 | 10:00 | 10:00 | |
| 11:00 | 11:00 | 11:00 | 11:00 | 11:00 | |
| 12:00 | 12:00 | 12:00 | 12:00 | 12:00 | |
| 1:00 | 1:00 | 1:00 | 1:00 | 1:00 | |
| 2:00 | 2:00 | 2:00 | 2:00 | 2:00 | SUNDAY ☐ |
| 3:00 | 3:00 | 3:00 | 3:00 | 3:00 | |
| 4:00 | 4:00 | 4:00 | 4:00 | 4:00 | |
| 5:00 | 5:00 | 5:00 | 5:00 | 5:00 | |
| 6:00 | 6:00 | 6:00 | 6:00 | 6:00 | |
| 7:00 | 7:00 | 7:00 | 7:00 | 7:00 | |

| Do. Call | Do. Call | Do. Call | Do. Call | Do. Call | Do. Call |
|---|---|---|---|---|---|

| $ Money in | $ Money in | $ Money in | $ Money in | $ Money in | $ Money in |
|---|---|---|---|---|---|

## Remembering Me

I am: _____

What I love about me is: _____

_____

What I am proud of this week is: _____

_____

## Weekly Goals:

1. _____ ○   3. _____ ○

2. _____ ○   4. _____ ○

## Not to Miss:

· ·

· ·

## Projects to Complete:

_____

_____

_____

_____

## Recipes to Try:

_____

_____

_____

_____

## To Beautify my Home:

_____

_____

_____

_____

## Call - Email - Social Media:

· ·

· ·

· ·

· ·

## To Do:

_____

_____

_____

_____

### Groceries:

_____

_____

_____

## To Buy:

· ·

· ·

· ·

## My Balanced Heart

KIND KIN DEED
FAMILY HOLIDAY
COUPLES DATES
FRIENDS
HAVING FUN TOGETHER
KIND KID DEED
MY FAMILY
BESTIES
SPOUSES FAMILY
KIDS & PETS
SPOUSE
GROWING
ME
ALONE TIME
READING
WORK
SELF CARE
MASSAGE
SAVINGS
EXERCISE
SPIRITUAL WELL BEING
CREATIVITY
INVESTING
MUSIC
CARDIO
MEDITATION
WEIGHT
DEEP BREATHING
YOGA & STRETCHING
WALKING
TIME IN NATURE
CONTRIBUTING TO OTHERS

## My Weekly Reflection

## What word best describes ME this week?

# My Authentic Heart Words

| | | | | | |
|---|---|---|---|---|---|
| Workout | Ⓐ Ⓒ | Ⓐ Ⓒ | Ⓐ Ⓒ | Ⓐ Ⓒ | Ⓐ Ⓒ | Ⓐ Ⓒ |

| | | | | | |
|---|---|---|---|---|---|
| Just for Me | ♥ | ♥ | ♥ | ♥ | ♥ |

Water

Wins ✓

Daily Happy Moment ☺

| **MONDAY** ☐ | **TUESDAY** ☐ | **WEDNESDAY** ☐ | **THURSDAY** ☐ | **FRIDAY** ☐ | **SATURDAY** ☐ |
|---|---|---|---|---|---|
| 7:00 | 7:00 | 7:00 | 7:00 | 7:00 | |
| 8:00 | 8:00 | 8:00 | 8:00 | 8:00 | |
| 9:00 | 9:00 | 9:00 | 9:00 | 9:00 | |
| 10:00 | 10:00 | 10:00 | 10:00 | 10:00 | |
| 11:00 | 11:00 | 11:00 | 11:00 | 11:00 | |
| 12:00 | 12:00 | 12:00 | 12:00 | 12:00 | |
| 1:00 | 1:00 | 1:00 | 1:00 | 1:00 | |
| 2:00 | 2:00 | 2:00 | 2:00 | 2:00 | **SUNDAY** ☐ |
| 3:00 | 3:00 | 3:00 | 3:00 | 3:00 | |
| 4:00 | 4:00 | 4:00 | 4:00 | 4:00 | |
| 5:00 | 5:00 | 5:00 | 5:00 | 5:00 | |
| 6:00 | 6:00 | 6:00 | 6:00 | 6:00 | |
| 7:00 | 7:00 | 7:00 | 7:00 | 7:00 | |

| Do. Call | Do. Call | Do. Call | Do. Call | Do. Call | Do. Call |
|---|---|---|---|---|---|
| | | | | | |

| $ Money in | $ Money in | $ Money in | $ Money in | $ Money in | $ Money in |
|---|---|---|---|---|---|
| | | | | | |

## Remembering Me

I am: _____

What I love about me is: _____
_____

What I am proud of this week is: _____
_____

## Weekly Goals:

1. _____ ○   3. _____ ○

2. _____ ○   4. _____ ○

## Not to Miss:

.                    .

.                    .

## Projects to Complete:

_____
_____
_____
_____

## Recipes to Try:

_____
_____
_____
_____

## To Beautify my Home:

_____
_____
_____
_____

## Call - Email - Social Media:

.              .

.              .

.              .

.              .

## To Do:

_____  _____
_____  _____
_____
_____
_____

## Groceries:

_____  _____  _____
_____  _____  _____
_____  _____  _____

## To Buy:

.              .

.              .

## My Balanced Heart

## My Weekly Reflection

## What word best describes ME this week?

# My Authentic Heart Words

|  |  |  |  |  |  |
|--|--|--|--|--|--|
|  |  |  |  |  |  |

| Workout | Ⓐ Ⓒ | Ⓐ Ⓒ | Ⓐ Ⓒ | Ⓐ Ⓒ | Ⓐ Ⓒ | Ⓐ Ⓒ |
|---------|------|------|------|------|------|------|
| Just for Me | ♥ | ♥ | ♥ | ♥ | ♥ | |
| Water | ⬚⬚⬚⬚⬚⬚ | ⬚⬚⬚⬚⬚⬚ | ⬚⬚⬚⬚⬚⬚ | ⬚⬚⬚⬚⬚⬚ | ⬚⬚⬚⬚⬚⬚ | ⬚⬚⬚⬚⬚⬚ |
| Wins ✓ | | | | | | |
| Daily Happy Moment ☺ | | | | | | |

## MONDAY ☐ | TUESDAY ☐ | WEDNESDAY ☐ | THURSDAY ☐ | FRIDAY ☐ | SATURDAY ☐

| MONDAY | TUESDAY | WEDNESDAY | THURSDAY | FRIDAY | SATURDAY |
|--------|---------|-----------|----------|--------|----------|
| 7:00 | 7:00 | 7:00 | 7:00 | 7:00 | |
| 8:00 | 8:00 | 8:00 | 8:00 | 8:00 | |
| 9:00 | 9:00 | 9:00 | 9:00 | 9:00 | |
| 10:00 | 10:00 | 10:00 | 10:00 | 10:00 | |
| 11:00 | 11:00 | 11:00 | 11:00 | 11:00 | |
| 12:00 | 12:00 | 12:00 | 12:00 | 12:00 | |
| 1:00 | 1:00 | 1:00 | 1:00 | 1:00 | |
| 2:00 | 2:00 | 2:00 | 2:00 | 2:00 | SUNDAY ☐ |
| 3:00 | 3:00 | 3:00 | 3:00 | 3:00 | |
| 4:00 | 4:00 | 4:00 | 4:00 | 4:00 | |
| 5:00 | 5:00 | 5:00 | 5:00 | 5:00 | |
| 6:00 | 6:00 | 6:00 | 6:00 | 6:00 | |
| 7:00 | 7:00 | 7:00 | 7:00 | 7:00 | |

| Do. Call | Do. Call | Do. Call | Do. Call | Do. Call | Do. Call |
|----------|----------|----------|----------|----------|----------|
| | | | | | |

| $ Money in | $ Money in | $ Money in | $ Money in | $ Money in | $ Money in |
|------------|------------|------------|------------|------------|------------|
| | | | | | |

## Remembering Me

I am: _____

What I love about me is: _____

_____

What I am proud of this week is: _____

_____

## Weekly Goals:

1. _____ ○   3. _____ ○

2. _____ ○   4. _____ ○

## Not to Miss:

· _____        · _____

· _____        · _____

## Projects to Complete:

_____
_____
_____
_____

## Recipes to Try:

_____
_____
_____
_____

## To Beautify my Home:

_____
_____
_____
_____

## Call - Email - Social Media:

· _____        · _____

· _____        · _____

· _____        · _____

· _____        · _____

## To Buy:

· _____        · _____

· _____        · _____

· _____        · _____

## To Do:

_____   _____
_____   _____
_____   _____

### Groceries:

_____   _____ _____
_____   _____ _____
_____   _____ _____
_____   _____ _____

## My Balanced Heart

FAMILY HOLIDAY · KIND KIN DEED · COUPLES DATES · FRIENDS · HAVING FUN TOGETHER · SPOUSES FAMILY · ALONE TIME · MASSAGE · CREATIVITY · MUSIC · MEDITATION · DEEP BREATHING · TIME IN NATURE · CONTRIBUTING TO OTHERS · WALKING · YOGA & STRETCHING · WEIGHT · CARDIO · INVESTING · SAVINGS · READING · GROWING · KIND KID DEED

MY FAMILY · BESTIES · KIDS & PETS · SPOUSE · ME · WORK · SELF CARE · EXERCISE · SPIRITUAL WELL BEING

## My Weekly Reflection

## What word best describes ME this week?

51

# My Authentic Heart Words

|  |  |  |  |  |  |
|---|---|---|---|---|---|
|  |  |  |  |  |  |

| | | | | | | |
|---|---|---|---|---|---|---|
| Workout | Ⓐ Ⓒ | Ⓐ Ⓒ | Ⓐ Ⓒ | Ⓐ Ⓒ | Ⓐ Ⓒ | Ⓐ Ⓒ |
| Just for Me | ♥ | ♥ | ♥ | ♥ | ♥ | |
| Water | ▭▭▭▭▭▭ | ▭▭▭▭▭▭ | ▭▭▭▭▭▭ | ▭▭▭▭▭▭ | ▭▭▭▭▭▭ | ▭▭▭▭▭▭ |
| Wins ✓ | | | | | | |
| Daily Happy Moment ☺ | | | | | | |

| MONDAY ☐ | TUESDAY ☐ | WEDNESDAY ☐ | THURSDAY ☐ | FRIDAY ☐ | SATURDAY ☐ |
|---|---|---|---|---|---|
| 7:00 | 7:00 | 7:00 | 7:00 | 7:00 | |
| 8:00 | 8:00 | 8:00 | 8:00 | 8:00 | |
| 9:00 | 9:00 | 9:00 | 9:00 | 9:00 | |
| 10:00 | 10:00 | 10:00 | 10:00 | 10:00 | |
| 11:00 | 11:00 | 11:00 | 11:00 | 11:00 | |
| 12:00 | 12:00 | 12:00 | 12:00 | 12:00 | |
| 1:00 | 1:00 | 1:00 | 1:00 | 1:00 | |
| 2:00 | 2:00 | 2:00 | 2:00 | 2:00 | SUNDAY ☐ |
| 3:00 | 3:00 | 3:00 | 3:00 | 3:00 | |
| 4:00 | 4:00 | 4:00 | 4:00 | 4:00 | |
| 5:00 | 5:00 | 5:00 | 5:00 | 5:00 | |
| 6:00 | 6:00 | 6:00 | 6:00 | 6:00 | |
| 7:00 | 7:00 | 7:00 | 7:00 | 7:00 | |

| Do. Call | Do. Call | Do. Call | Do. Call | Do. Call | Do. Call |
|---|---|---|---|---|---|
| | | | | | |

| $ Money in | $ Money in | $ Money in | $ Money in | $ Money in | $ Money in |
|---|---|---|---|---|---|
| | | | | | |

## Remembering Me

I am: _____

What I love about me is: _____

_____

What I am proud of this week is: _____

_____

## Weekly Goals:

1. _____ ○   3. _____ ○

2. _____ ○   4. _____ ○

## Not to Miss:

·       ·

·       ·

## Projects to Complete:

_____
_____
_____
_____

## Recipes to Try:

_____
_____
_____
_____

## To Beautify my Home:

_____
_____
_____
_____

## Call - Email - Social Media:

·       ·

·       ·

·       ·

·       ·

## To Do:

_____  _____
_____  _____
_____

## Groceries:

_____  _____  _____
_____  _____  _____
_____  _____  _____

## To Buy:

·       ·

·       ·

·       ·

## My Balanced Heart

KIND KIN DEED
FAMILY HOLIDAY
COUPLES DATES
FRIENDS
HAVING FUN TOGETHER
KIND KID DEED
MY FAMILY
BESTIES
SPOUSES FAMILY
KIDS & PETS
SPOUSE
GROWING
ME
SELF CARE
ALONE TIME
READING
WORK
MASSAGE
SAVINGS
SPIRITUAL WELL BEING
CREATIVITY
INVESTING
EXERCISE
MUSIC
CARDIO
MEDITATION
WEIGHT
DEEP BREATHING
YOGA & STRETCHING
WALKING
TIME IN NATURE
CONTRIBUTING TO OTHERS

## My Weekly Reflection

## What word best describes ME this week?

# My Authentic Heart Words

| | | | | | |
|---|---|---|---|---|---|
| | | | | | |

| | | | | | | |
|---|---|---|---|---|---|---|
| Workout | Ⓐ Ⓒ | Ⓐ Ⓒ | Ⓐ Ⓒ | Ⓐ Ⓒ | Ⓐ Ⓒ | Ⓐ Ⓒ |
| Just for Me | ♥ | ♥ | ♥ | ♥ | ♥ | |
| Water | ⬜⬜⬜⬜⬜⬜ | ⬜⬜⬜⬜⬜⬜ | ⬜⬜⬜⬜⬜⬜ | ⬜⬜⬜⬜⬜⬜ | ⬜⬜⬜⬜⬜⬜ | ⬜⬜⬜⬜⬜⬜ |
| Wins ✓ | | | | | | |
| Daily Happy Moment ☺ | | | | | | |

| MONDAY ☐ | TUESDAY ☐ | WEDNESDAY ☐ | THURSDAY ☐ | FRIDAY ☐ | SATURDAY ☐ |
|---|---|---|---|---|---|
| 7:00 | 7:00 | 7:00 | 7:00 | 7:00 | |
| 8:00 | 8:00 | 8:00 | 8:00 | 8:00 | |
| 9:00 | 9:00 | 9:00 | 9:00 | 9:00 | |
| 10:00 | 10:00 | 10:00 | 10:00 | 10:00 | |
| 11:00 | 11:00 | 11:00 | 11:00 | 11:00 | |
| 12:00 | 12:00 | 12:00 | 12:00 | 12:00 | |
| 1:00 | 1:00 | 1:00 | 1:00 | 1:00 | |
| 2:00 | 2:00 | 2:00 | 2:00 | 2:00 | SUNDAY ☐ |
| 3:00 | 3:00 | 3:00 | 3:00 | 3:00 | |
| 4:00 | 4:00 | 4:00 | 4:00 | 4:00 | |
| 5:00 | 5:00 | 5:00 | 5:00 | 5:00 | |
| 6:00 | 6:00 | 6:00 | 6:00 | 6:00 | |
| 7:00 | 7:00 | 7:00 | 7:00 | 7:00 | |

| Do. Call | Do. Call | Do. Call | Do. Call | Do. Call | Do. Call |
|---|---|---|---|---|---|

| $ Money in | $ Money in | $ Money in | $ Money in | $ Money in | $ Money in |
|---|---|---|---|---|---|

## Remembering Me

I am: _____

What I love about me is: _____

_____

What I am proud of this week is: _____

_____

## Weekly Goals:

1. _____ ○   3. _____ ○

2. _____ ○   4. _____ ○

## Not to Miss:

. _____   . _____

. _____   . _____

## Projects to Complete:

_____

_____

_____

_____

## Recipes to Try:

_____

_____

_____

_____

## To Beautify my Home:

_____

_____

_____

_____

## Call - Email - Social Media:

. _____   . _____

. _____   . _____

. _____   . _____

. _____   . _____

## To Do:

_____   _____

_____   _____

_____   

_____   ### Groceries:

_____   _____  _____

## To Buy:

. _____   . _____

. _____   . _____

. _____   . _____

### My Balanced Heart

KIND KIN DEED, FAMILY HOLIDAY, COUPLES DATES, FRIENDS, HAVING FUN TOGETHER, MY FAMILY, BESTIES, SPOUSES FAMILY, KIND KID DEED, KIDS & PETS, SPOUSE, GROWING, ME, SELF CARE, ALONE TIME, READING, WORK, MASSAGE, SAVINGS, EXERCISE, SPIRITUAL WELL BEING, CREATIVITY, INVESTING, MUSIC, CARDIO, MEDITATION, WEIGHT, YOGA & STRETCHING, WALKING, CONTRIBUTING TO OTHERS, TIME IN NATURE, DEEP BREATHING

### My Weekly Reflection

### What word best describes ME this week?

## This Month ♥

### Goals to Complete:

1. _____ ○
2. _____ ○
3. _____ ○
4. _____ ○
5. _____ ○

### Places to Explore:

_____
_____
_____
_____
_____

### To Buy:

· _____ · _____
· _____ · _____
· _____ · _____

### Not to Miss:

· _____ · _____
· _____ · _____
· _____ · _____

### Favorite Books I am Reading:

· _____ · _____
· _____ · _____

## Month: _____

| SUNDAY | MONDAY | TUESDAY |
|--------|--------|---------|
|        |        |         |
|        |        |         |
|        |        |         |
|        |        |         |
|        |        |         |

## ♥ PLAN OF ACTION

### Work:

○ _____
○ _____
○ _____
○ _____
○ _____
○ _____
○ _____
○ _____

### Personal:

○ _____
○ _____
○ _____
○ _____
○ _____
○ _____
○ _____
○ _____

### Misc:

○ _____
○ _____
○ _____
○ _____
○ _____
○ _____
○ _____
○ _____

*"One shoe can change your life."* ~ Cinderella

## My Accomplishments this Month

| WEDNESDAY | THURSDAY | FRIDAY | SATURDAY |
|---|---|---|---|
| | | | |
| | | | |
| | | | |
| | | | |
| | | | |

**Improvements In My Life:**

.

.

.

.

**Good Deeds Done:**

.

.

.

.

**Fun and Spontaneous:**

.

.

.

**I Treated Myself To:**

.

.

.

.

**New Experiences:**

.

.

.

.

### What made my ♥ happy this month...

With gratitude & love, thank you.

### My Manifestation List:

| CLAIM AS TRUE | DATE RECEIVED |
|---|---|
| 1. _____ | _____ |
| 2. _____ | _____ |
| 3. _____ | _____ |
| 4. _____ | _____ |
| 5. _____ | _____ |

# $ Keeping Track of the Flow of it All

**Month:** _____

| DATES + DETAILS | MONEY IN | SAVINGS | SHARING WITH OTHERS | INSURANCE + HEALTH EXPENSES | HOUSE EXPENSES | GROCERIES | TRANSPORTATION EXPENSES | ENTERTAINMENT + FUN EXPENSES | HOLIDAY EXPENSES | PERSONAL EXPENSES | DINING OUT | MISC |
|---|---|---|---|---|---|---|---|---|---|---|---|---|
|  |  |  |  |  |  |  |  |  |  |  |  |  |
|  |  |  |  |  |  |  |  |  |  |  |  |  |
|  |  |  |  |  |  |  |  |  |  |  |  |  |
|  |  |  |  |  |  |  |  |  |  |  |  |  |
|  |  |  |  |  |  |  |  |  |  |  |  |  |
|  |  |  |  |  |  |  |  |  |  |  |  |  |
|  |  |  |  |  |  |  |  |  |  |  |  |  |
|  |  |  |  |  |  |  |  |  |  |  |  |  |
|  |  |  |  |  |  |  |  |  |  |  |  |  |
|  |  |  |  |  |  |  |  |  |  |  |  |  |
|  |  |  |  |  |  |  |  |  |  |  |  |  |
|  |  |  |  |  |  |  |  |  |  |  |  |  |
| $ TOTALS |  |  |  |  |  |  |  |  |  |  |  |  |

# My Journaling Space ♥

# My Authentic Heart Words

| | | | | | |
|---|---|---|---|---|---|
| | | | | | |

| | | | | | | |
|---|---|---|---|---|---|---|
| Workout | Ⓐ Ⓒ | Ⓐ Ⓒ | Ⓐ Ⓒ | Ⓐ Ⓒ | Ⓐ Ⓒ | Ⓐ Ⓒ |
| Just for Me | ♥ | ♥ | ♥ | ♥ | ♥ | |
| Water | ▭▭▭▭▭▭ | ▭▭▭▭▭▭ | ▭▭▭▭▭▭ | ▭▭▭▭▭▭ | ▭▭▭▭▭▭ | ▭▭▭▭▭▭ |
| Wins ✓ | | | | | | |
| Daily Happy Moment ☺ | | | | | | |

| MONDAY ☐ | TUESDAY ☐ | WEDNESDAY ☐ | THURSDAY ☐ | FRIDAY ☐ | SATURDAY ☐ |
|---|---|---|---|---|---|
| 7:00 | 7:00 | 7:00 | 7:00 | 7:00 | |
| 8:00 | 8:00 | 8:00 | 8:00 | 8:00 | |
| 9:00 | 9:00 | 9:00 | 9:00 | 9:00 | |
| 10:00 | 10:00 | 10:00 | 10:00 | 10:00 | |
| 11:00 | 11:00 | 11:00 | 11:00 | 11:00 | |
| 12:00 | 12:00 | 12:00 | 12:00 | 12:00 | |
| 1:00 | 1:00 | 1:00 | 1:00 | 1:00 | |
| 2:00 | 2:00 | 2:00 | 2:00 | 2:00 | SUNDAY ☐ |
| 3:00 | 3:00 | 3:00 | 3:00 | 3:00 | |
| 4:00 | 4:00 | 4:00 | 4:00 | 4:00 | |
| 5:00 | 5:00 | 5:00 | 5:00 | 5:00 | |
| 6:00 | 6:00 | 6:00 | 6:00 | 6:00 | |
| 7:00 | 7:00 | 7:00 | 7:00 | 7:00 | |

| Do. Call | Do. Call | Do. Call | Do. Call | Do. Call | Do. Call |
|---|---|---|---|---|---|
| | | | | | |

| $ Money in | $ Money in | $ Money in | $ Money in | $ Money in | $ Money in |
|---|---|---|---|---|---|
| | | | | | |

## Remembering Me

I am: _____

What I love about me is: _____

_____

What I am proud of this week is: _____

_____

## Weekly Goals:

1. _____ ○   3. _____ ○

2. _____ ○   4. _____ ○

## Not to Miss:

·                    ·

·                    ·

## Projects to Complete:

_____

_____

_____

_____

## Recipes to Try:

_____

_____

_____

_____

## To Beautify my Home:

_____

_____

_____

_____

## Call - Email - Social Media:

·                    ·

·                    ·

·                    ·

·                    ·

## To Buy:

·                    ·

·                    ·

·                    ·

## To Do:

_____   _____

_____   _____

_____   

### Groceries:

_____   _____ _____

_____   _____ _____

_____   _____ _____

_____   _____ _____

*My Balanced Heart*

KIND KIN DEED
FAMILY HOLIDAY
COUPLES DATES
FRIENDS
HAVING FUN TOGETHER
MY FAMILY
BESTIES
SPOUSES FAMILY
KIND KID DEED
KIDS & PETS
SPOUSE
GROWING
ME
ALONE TIME
READING
WORK
SELF CARE
MASSAGE
SAVINGS
EXERCISE
SPIRITUAL WELL BEING
CREATIVITY
INVESTING
MUSIC
CARDIO
MEDITATION
WEIGHT
YOGA & STRETCHING
WALKING
CONTRIBUTING TO OTHERS
TIME IN NATURE
DEEP BREATHING

*My Weekly Reflection*

## What word best describes ME this week?

# My Authentic Heart Words

| | | | | | |
|---|---|---|---|---|---|

| Workout | Ⓐ Ⓒ | Ⓐ Ⓒ | Ⓐ Ⓒ | Ⓐ Ⓒ | Ⓐ Ⓒ | Ⓐ Ⓒ |
|---|---|---|---|---|---|---|
| Just for Me | ♥ | ♥ | ♥ | ♥ | ♥ | |
| Water | ▽▽▽▽▽▽ | ▽▽▽▽▽ | ▽▽▽▽▽ | ▽▽▽▽▽ | ▽▽▽▽▽ | ▽▽▽▽▽ |
| Wins ✓ | | | | | | |
| Daily Happy Moment ☺ | | | | | | |

| MONDAY ☐ | TUESDAY ☐ | WEDNESDAY ☐ | THURSDAY ☐ | FRIDAY ☐ | SATURDAY ☐ |
|---|---|---|---|---|---|
| 7:00 | 7:00 | 7:00 | 7:00 | 7:00 | |
| 8:00 | 8:00 | 8:00 | 8:00 | 8:00 | |
| 9:00 | 9:00 | 9:00 | 9:00 | 9:00 | |
| 10:00 | 10:00 | 10:00 | 10:00 | 10:00 | |
| 11:00 | 11:00 | 11:00 | 11:00 | 11:00 | |
| 12:00 | 12:00 | 12:00 | 12:00 | 12:00 | |
| 1:00 | 1:00 | 1:00 | 1:00 | 1:00 | |
| 2:00 | 2:00 | 2:00 | 2:00 | 2:00 | SUNDAY ☐ |
| 3:00 | 3:00 | 3:00 | 3:00 | 3:00 | |
| 4:00 | 4:00 | 4:00 | 4:00 | 4:00 | |
| 5:00 | 5:00 | 5:00 | 5:00 | 5:00 | |
| 6:00 | 6:00 | 6:00 | 6:00 | 6:00 | |
| 7:00 | 7:00 | 7:00 | 7:00 | 7:00 | |

| Do. Call | Do. Call | Do. Call | Do. Call | Do. Call | Do. Call |
|---|---|---|---|---|---|
| | | | | | |

| $ Money in | $ Money in | $ Money in | $ Money in | $ Money in | $ Money in |
|---|---|---|---|---|---|
| | | | | | |

## Remembering Me

I am: _____

What I love about me is: _____

_____

What I am proud of this week is: _____

_____

## Weekly Goals:

1. _____ ○   3. _____ ○

2. _____ ○   4. _____ ○

## Not to Miss:
· _____   · _____

· _____   · _____

## Projects to Complete:
_____
_____
_____
_____

## Recipes to Try:
_____
_____
_____
_____

## To Beautify my Home:
_____
_____
_____
_____

## Call - Email - Social Media:
· _____   · _____
· _____   · _____
· _____   · _____
· _____   · _____

## To Do:
_____   _____
_____   _____
_____   
### Groceries:
_____   _____   _____
_____   _____   _____
_____   _____   _____

## To Buy:
· _____   · _____
· _____   · _____
· _____   · _____

### My Balanced Heart

KIND KIN DEED
FAMILY HOLIDAY
COUPLES DATES
FRIENDS
HAVING FUN TOGETHER
KIND KID DEED
MY FAMILY
BESTIES
SPOUSES FAMILY
GROWING
KIDS & PETS
SPOUSE
READING
WORK
ME
SELF CARE
ALONE TIME
SAVINGS
EXERCISE
SPIRITUAL WELL BEING
MASSAGE
INVESTING
CREATIVITY
CARDIO
MUSIC
WEIGHT
MEDITATION
YOGA & STRETCHING
WALKING
DEEP BREATHING
CONTRIBUTING TO OTHERS
TIME IN NATURE

### My Weekly Reflection

### What word best describes ME this week?

# My Authentic Heart Words

| | | | | | |
|---|---|---|---|---|---|
| | | | | | |

| | | | | | | |
|---|---|---|---|---|---|---|
| Workout | Ⓐ Ⓒ | Ⓐ Ⓒ | Ⓐ Ⓒ | Ⓐ Ⓒ | Ⓐ Ⓒ | Ⓐ Ⓒ |
| Just for Me | ♥ | ♥ | ♥ | ♥ | ♥ | |
| Water | ▭▭▭▭▭▭ | ▭▭▭▭▭▭ | ▭▭▭▭▭▭ | ▭▭▭▭▭▭ | ▭▭▭▭▭▭ | ▭▭▭▭▭▭ |
| Wins ✓ | | | | | | |
| Daily Happy Moment ☺ | | | | | | |

| MONDAY ☐ | TUESDAY ☐ | WEDNESDAY ☐ | THURSDAY ☐ | FRIDAY ☐ | SATURDAY ☐ |
|---|---|---|---|---|---|
| 7:00 | 7:00 | 7:00 | 7:00 | 7:00 | |
| 8:00 | 8:00 | 8:00 | 8:00 | 8:00 | |
| 9:00 | 9:00 | 9:00 | 9:00 | 9:00 | |
| 10:00 | 10:00 | 10:00 | 10:00 | 10:00 | |
| 11:00 | 11:00 | 11:00 | 11:00 | 11:00 | |
| 12:00 | 12:00 | 12:00 | 12:00 | 12:00 | |
| 1:00 | 1:00 | 1:00 | 1:00 | 1:00 | |
| 2:00 | 2:00 | 2:00 | 2:00 | 2:00 | SUNDAY ☐ |
| 3:00 | 3:00 | 3:00 | 3:00 | 3:00 | |
| 4:00 | 4:00 | 4:00 | 4:00 | 4:00 | |
| 5:00 | 5:00 | 5:00 | 5:00 | 5:00 | |
| 6:00 | 6:00 | 6:00 | 6:00 | 6:00 | |
| 7:00 | 7:00 | 7:00 | 7:00 | 7:00 | |

| Do. Call | Do. Call | Do. Call | Do. Call | Do. Call | Do. Call |
|---|---|---|---|---|---|
| | | | | | |

| $ Money in | $ Money in | $ Money in | $ Money in | $ Money in | $ Money in |
|---|---|---|---|---|---|
| | | | | | |

## Remembering Me

I am: _____

What I love about me is: _____

_____

What I am proud of this week is: _____

_____

## Weekly Goals:

1. _____ ○   3. _____ ○

2. _____ ○   4. _____ ○

## Not to Miss:

- · ·
- · ·

## Projects to Complete:

_____

_____

_____

_____

## Recipes to Try:

_____

_____

_____

_____

## To Beautify my Home:

_____

_____

_____

_____

## Call - Email - Social Media:

- · ·
- · ·
- · ·
- · ·

## To Buy:

- · ·
- · ·
- · ·

## To Do:

_____   _____

_____   _____

_____   

### Groceries:

_____   _____   _____

_____   _____   _____

_____   _____   _____

_____   _____   _____

## My Balanced Heart

FAMILY HOLIDAY · KIND KIN DEED · COUPLES DATES · FRIENDS · HAVING FUN TOGETHER · SPOUSES FAMILY · KIND KID DEED · MY FAMILY · BESTIES · SPOUSE · ALONE TIME · GROWING · KIDS & PETS · SELF CARE · MASSAGE · READING · ME · WORK · CREATIVITY · SAVINGS · EXERCISE · SPIRITUAL WELL BEING · MUSIC · INVESTING · MEDITATION · CARDIO · WEIGHT · DEEP BREATHING · YOGA & STRETCHING · WALKING · TIME IN NATURE · CONTRIBUTING TO OTHERS

## My Weekly Reflection

## What word best describes ME this week?

# My Authentic Heart Words

| | | | | | |
|---|---|---|---|---|---|
| | | | | | |

| | | | | | | |
|---|---|---|---|---|---|---|
| Workout | Ⓐ Ⓒ | Ⓐ Ⓒ | Ⓐ Ⓒ | Ⓐ Ⓒ | Ⓐ Ⓒ | Ⓐ Ⓒ |
| Just for Me | ♥ | ♥ | ♥ | ♥ | ♥ | |
| Water | ▢▢▢▢▢▢ | ▢▢▢▢▢▢ | ▢▢▢▢▢▢ | ▢▢▢▢▢▢ | ▢▢▢▢▢▢ | ▢▢▢▢▢▢ |
| Wins ✓ | | | | | | |
| Daily Happy Moment ☺ | | | | | | |

| MONDAY ▢ | TUESDAY ▢ | WEDNESDAY ▢ | THURSDAY ▢ | FRIDAY ▢ | SATURDAY ▢ |
|---|---|---|---|---|---|
| 7:00 | 7:00 | 7:00 | 7:00 | 7:00 | |
| 8:00 | 8:00 | 8:00 | 8:00 | 8:00 | |
| 9:00 | 9:00 | 9:00 | 9:00 | 9:00 | |
| 10:00 | 10:00 | 10:00 | 10:00 | 10:00 | |
| 11:00 | 11:00 | 11:00 | 11:00 | 11:00 | |
| 12:00 | 12:00 | 12:00 | 12:00 | 12:00 | |
| 1:00 | 1:00 | 1:00 | 1:00 | 1:00 | |
| 2:00 | 2:00 | 2:00 | 2:00 | 2:00 | SUNDAY ▢ |
| 3:00 | 3:00 | 3:00 | 3:00 | 3:00 | |
| 4:00 | 4:00 | 4:00 | 4:00 | 4:00 | |
| 5:00 | 5:00 | 5:00 | 5:00 | 5:00 | |
| 6:00 | 6:00 | 6:00 | 6:00 | 6:00 | |
| 7:00 | 7:00 | 7:00 | 7:00 | 7:00 | |

| Do. Call | Do. Call | Do. Call | Do. Call | Do. Call | Do. Call |
|---|---|---|---|---|---|
| | | | | | |

| $ Money in | $ Money in | $ Money in | $ Money in | $ Money in | $ Money in |
|---|---|---|---|---|---|
| | | | | | |

## Remembering Me

I am: _____

What I love about me is: _____

_____

What I am proud of this week is: _____

_____

## Weekly Goals:

1. _____ ○   3. _____ ○

2. _____ ○   4. _____ ○

## Not to Miss:

·                    ·

·                    ·

## Projects to Complete:

_____

_____

_____

_____

## Recipes to Try:

_____

_____

_____

## To Beautify my Home:

_____

_____

_____

## Call - Email - Social Media:

·                    ·

·                    ·

·                    ·

·                    ·

## To Do:

_____   _____

_____   _____

_____   ## Groceries:

_____   _____  _____

## To Buy:

·                    ·

·                    ·

My Balanced Heart

## My Weekly Reflection

## What word best describes ME this week?

# My Authentic Heart Words

|  |  |  |  |  |  |
|---|---|---|---|---|---|
|  |  |  |  |  |  |

| | | | | | |
|---|---|---|---|---|---|
| Workout | Ⓐ Ⓒ | Ⓐ Ⓒ | Ⓐ Ⓒ | Ⓐ Ⓒ | Ⓐ Ⓒ | Ⓐ Ⓒ |

| Just for Me | ♥ | ♥ | ♥ | ♥ | ♥ |

Water

☐☐☐☐☐☐☐  ☐☐☐☐☐☐☐  ☐☐☐☐☐☐☐  ☐☐☐☐☐☐☐  ☐☐☐☐☐☐☐  ☐☐☐☐☐☐☐

Wins ✓

Daily Happy Moment ☺

| **MONDAY** ☐ | **TUESDAY** ☐ | **WEDNESDAY** ☐ | **THURSDAY** ☐ | **FRIDAY** ☐ | **SATURDAY** ☐ |
|---|---|---|---|---|---|
| 7:00 | 7:00 | 7:00 | 7:00 | 7:00 | |
| 8:00 | 8:00 | 8:00 | 8:00 | 8:00 | |
| 9:00 | 9:00 | 9:00 | 9:00 | 9:00 | |
| 10:00 | 10:00 | 10:00 | 10:00 | 10:00 | |
| 11:00 | 11:00 | 11:00 | 11:00 | 11:00 | |
| 12:00 | 12:00 | 12:00 | 12:00 | 12:00 | |
| 1:00 | 1:00 | 1:00 | 1:00 | 1:00 | |
| 2:00 | 2:00 | 2:00 | 2:00 | 2:00 | **SUNDAY** ☐ |
| 3:00 | 3:00 | 3:00 | 3:00 | 3:00 | |
| 4:00 | 4:00 | 4:00 | 4:00 | 4:00 | |
| 5:00 | 5:00 | 5:00 | 5:00 | 5:00 | |
| 6:00 | 6:00 | 6:00 | 6:00 | 6:00 | |
| 7:00 | 7:00 | 7:00 | 7:00 | 7:00 | |

| Do. Call | Do. Call | Do. Call | Do. Call | Do. Call | Do. Call |
|---|---|---|---|---|---|
| | | | | | |

| $ Money in | $ Money in | $ Money in | $ Money in | $ Money in | $ Money in |
|---|---|---|---|---|---|
| | | | | | |

## Remembering Me

I am: _____

What I love about me is: _____

_____

What I am proud of this week is: _____

_____

## Weekly Goals:

1. _____ ○    3. _____ ○

2. _____ ○    4. _____ ○

## Not to Miss:

· _____    · _____

· _____    · _____

## Projects to Complete:

_____

_____

_____

_____

## Recipes to Try:

_____

_____

_____

_____

## To Beautify my Home:

_____

_____

_____

_____

## Call - Email - Social Media:

· _____    · _____

· _____    · _____

· _____    · _____

· _____    · _____

## To Buy:

· _____    · _____

· _____    · _____

## To Do:

_____    _____

_____    _____

_____    

_____    ## Groceries:

_____    _____  _____

_____    _____  _____

_____    _____  _____

_____    _____  _____

### My Balanced Heart

FAMILY HOLIDAY · KIND KIN DEED · COUPLES DATES · FRIENDS · HAVING FUN TOGETHER · SPOUSES FAMILY · KIND KID DEED · MY FAMILY · BESTIES · SPOUSE · ALONE TIME · GROWING · KIDS & PETS · ME · SELF CARE · MASSAGE · READING · WORK · SPIRITUAL WELL BEING · CREATIVITY · SAVINGS · EXERCISE · MUSIC · INVESTING · MEDITATION · CARDIO · DEEP BREATHING · WEIGHT · TIME IN NATURE · YOGA & STRETCHING · WALKING · CONTRIBUTING TO OTHERS

### My Weekly Reflection

## What word best describes ME this week?

## This Month ♥

### Goals to Complete:

1. _____ ○
2. _____ ○
3. _____ ○
4. _____ ○
5. _____ ○

### Places to Explore:

_____
_____
_____
_____
_____

### To Buy:

·          ·
·          ·
·          ·

### Not to Miss:

·          ·
·          ·
·          ·

### Favorite Books I am Reading:

·          ·
·          ·

## Month: _____

| SUNDAY | MONDAY | TUESDAY |
|---|---|---|
|  |  |  |
|  |  |  |
|  |  |  |
|  |  |  |
|  |  |  |

## ♥ PLAN OF ACTION

### Work:

○ _____
○ _____
○ _____
○ _____
○ _____
○ _____
○ _____
○ _____

### Personal:

○ _____
○ _____
○ _____
○ _____
○ _____
○ _____
○ _____
○ _____

### Misc:

○ _____
○ _____
○ _____
○ _____
○ _____
○ _____
○ _____
○ _____

*"Happiness is not a state to arrive at, but*
*a moment of traveling."* ~ *Margaret Lee*

| WEDNESDAY | THURSDAY | FRIDAY | SATURDAY |
|-----------|----------|--------|----------|
|           |          |        |          |
|           |          |        |          |
|           |          |        |          |
|           |          |        |          |
|           |          |        |          |

## What made my ♥ happy this month...

_____

_____

_____

_____

_____

_____

With gratitude & love, thank you.

## My Accomplishments this Month

### Improvements In My Life:

.

.

.

.

### Good Deeds Done:

.

.

.

.

### Fun and Spontaneous:

.

.

.

### I Treated Myself To:

.

.

.

.

### New Experiences:

.

.

.

.

### My Manifestation List:

| CLAIM AS TRUE | DATE RECEIVED |
|---------------|---------------|
| 1. _____ | _____ |
| 2. _____ | _____ |
| 3. _____ | _____ |
| 4. _____ | _____ |
| 5. _____ | _____ |

# $ Keeping Track of the Flow of it All

**Month:** _____

| DATES + DETAILS | MONEY IN | SAVINGS | SHARING WITH OTHERS | INSURANCE + HEALTH EXPENSES | HOUSE EXPENSES | GROCERIES | TRANSPORTATION EXPENSES | ENTERTAINMENT + FUN EXPENSES | HOLIDAY EXPENSES | PERSONAL EXPENSES | DINING OUT | MISC |
|---|---|---|---|---|---|---|---|---|---|---|---|---|
| | | | | | | | | | | | | |
| | | | | | | | | | | | | |
| | | | | | | | | | | | | |
| | | | | | | | | | | | | |
| | | | | | | | | | | | | |
| | | | | | | | | | | | | |
| | | | | | | | | | | | | |
| | | | | | | | | | | | | |
| | | | | | | | | | | | | |
| | | | | | | | | | | | | |
| | | | | | | | | | | | | |
| | | | | | | | | | | | | |
| | | | | | | | | | | | | |
| | | | | | | | | | | | | |
| | | | | | | | | | | | | |
| $ TOTALS | | | | | | | | | | | | |

# My Journaling Space ♥

# My Authentic Heart Words

| | | | | | |
|---|---|---|---|---|---|
| | | | | | |

| | | | | | | |
|---|---|---|---|---|---|---|
| Workout Ⓐ Ⓒ | | Ⓐ Ⓒ | Ⓐ Ⓒ | Ⓐ Ⓒ | Ⓐ Ⓒ | Ⓐ Ⓒ |
| Just for Me | ♥ | ♥ | ♥ | ♥ | ♥ | |
| Water | | | | | | |
| Wins ✓ | | | | | | |
| Daily Happy Moment ☺ | | | | | | |

| MONDAY ☐ | TUESDAY ☐ | WEDNESDAY ☐ | THURSDAY ☐ | FRIDAY ☐ | SATURDAY ☐ |
|---|---|---|---|---|---|
| 7:00 | 7:00 | 7:00 | 7:00 | 7:00 | |
| 8:00 | 8:00 | 8:00 | 8:00 | 8:00 | |
| 9:00 | 9:00 | 9:00 | 9:00 | 9:00 | |
| 10:00 | 10:00 | 10:00 | 10:00 | 10:00 | |
| 11:00 | 11:00 | 11:00 | 11:00 | 11:00 | |
| 12:00 | 12:00 | 12:00 | 12:00 | 12:00 | |
| 1:00 | 1:00 | 1:00 | 1:00 | 1:00 | |
| 2:00 | 2:00 | 2:00 | 2:00 | 2:00 | SUNDAY ☐ |
| 3:00 | 3:00 | 3:00 | 3:00 | 3:00 | |
| 4:00 | 4:00 | 4:00 | 4:00 | 4:00 | |
| 5:00 | 5:00 | 5:00 | 5:00 | 5:00 | |
| 6:00 | 6:00 | 6:00 | 6:00 | 6:00 | |
| 7:00 | 7:00 | 7:00 | 7:00 | 7:00 | |

| Do. Call | Do. Call | Do. Call | Do. Call | Do. Call | Do. Call |
|---|---|---|---|---|---|
| | | | | | |

| $ Money in | $ Money in | $ Money in | $ Money in | $ Money in | $ Money in |
|---|---|---|---|---|---|
| | | | | | |

## Remembering Me

I am: _____

What I love about me is: _____

_____

What I am proud of this week is: _____

_____

## Weekly Goals:

1. _____ ○   3. _____ ○

2. _____ ○   4. _____ ○

## Not to Miss:

· 

· 

· 

· 

## Projects to Complete:

_____

_____

_____

_____

## Recipes to Try:

_____

_____

_____

_____

## To Beautify my Home:

_____

_____

_____

_____

## Call - Email - Social Media:

· 

· 

· 

· 

· 

· 

· 

· 

## To Buy:

· 

· 

· 

· 

· 

· 

## To Do:

_____

_____

_____

_____

_____

## Groceries:

_____

_____

_____

_____

## My Balanced Heart

KIND KIN DEED
FAMILY HOLIDAY
COUPLES DATES
FRIENDS
HAVING FUN TOGETHER
KIND KID DEED
MY FAMILY
BESTIES
SPOUSES FAMILY
KIDS & PETS
SPOUSE
GROWING
ME
SELF CARE
ALONE TIME
READING
WORK
MASSAGE
SAVINGS
SELF CARE
CREATIVITY
INVESTING
EXERCISE
SPIRITUAL WELL BEING
MUSIC
CARDIO
MEDITATION
WEIGHT
DEEP BREATHING
YOGA & STRETCHING
WALKING
TIME IN NATURE
CONTRIBUTING TO OTHERS

## My Weekly Reflection

## What word best describes ME this week?

# My Authentic Heart Words

| | | | | | |
|---|---|---|---|---|---|
| | | | | | |

| | | | | | | |
|---|---|---|---|---|---|---|
| Workout | Ⓐ Ⓒ | Ⓐ Ⓒ | Ⓐ Ⓒ | Ⓐ Ⓒ | Ⓐ Ⓒ | Ⓐ Ⓒ |
| Just for Me | ♥ | ♥ | ♥ | ♥ | ♥ | |
| Water | ⊔⊔⊔⊔⊔⊔ | ⊔⊔⊔⊔⊔⊔ | ⊔⊔⊔⊔⊔⊔ | ⊔⊔⊔⊔⊔⊔ | ⊔⊔⊔⊔⊔⊔ | ⊔⊔⊔⊔⊔⊔ |
| Wins ✓ | | | | | | |
| Daily Happy Moment ☺ | | | | | | |

| MONDAY ☐ | TUESDAY ☐ | WEDNESDAY ☐ | THURSDAY ☐ | FRIDAY ☐ | SATURDAY ☐ |
|---|---|---|---|---|---|
| 7:00 | 7:00 | 7:00 | 7:00 | 7:00 | |
| 8:00 | 8:00 | 8:00 | 8:00 | 8:00 | |
| 9:00 | 9:00 | 9:00 | 9:00 | 9:00 | |
| 10:00 | 10:00 | 10:00 | 10:00 | 10:00 | |
| 11:00 | 11:00 | 11:00 | 11:00 | 11:00 | |
| 12:00 | 12:00 | 12:00 | 12:00 | 12:00 | |
| 1:00 | 1:00 | 1:00 | 1:00 | 1:00 | |
| 2:00 | 2:00 | 2:00 | 2:00 | 2:00 | SUNDAY ☐ |
| 3:00 | 3:00 | 3:00 | 3:00 | 3:00 | |
| 4:00 | 4:00 | 4:00 | 4:00 | 4:00 | |
| 5:00 | 5:00 | 5:00 | 5:00 | 5:00 | |
| 6:00 | 6:00 | 6:00 | 6:00 | 6:00 | |
| 7:00 | 7:00 | 7:00 | 7:00 | 7:00 | |

| Do. Call | Do. Call | Do. Call | Do. Call | Do. Call | Do. Call |
|---|---|---|---|---|---|
| | | | | | |

| $ Money in | $ Money in | $ Money in | $ Money in | $ Money in | $ Money in |
|---|---|---|---|---|---|
| | | | | | |

## Remembering Me

I am: _____

What I love about me is: _____

_____

What I am proud of this week is: _____

_____

## Weekly Goals:

1. _____ ○   3. _____ ○

2. _____ ○   4. _____ ○

## Not to Miss:

• _____   • _____

• _____   • _____

## Projects to Complete:

_____

_____

_____

_____

## Recipes to Try:

_____

_____

_____

## To Beautify my Home:

_____

_____

_____

## Call - Email - Social Media:

• _____   • _____

• _____   • _____

• _____   • _____

• _____   • _____

## To Do:

_____   _____

_____   _____

_____   _____

### Groceries:

_____   _____   _____

_____   _____   _____

_____   _____   _____

_____   _____   _____

## To Buy:

• _____   • _____

• _____   • _____

• _____   • _____

*My Balanced Heart*

KIND KIN DEED
FAMILY HOLIDAY
COUPLES DATES
FRIENDS
HAVING FUN TOGETHER
MY FAMILY
BESTIES
SPOUSES FAMILY
KIND KID DEED
KIDS & PETS
SPOUSE
GROWING
ME
SELF CARE
ALONE TIME
READING
WORK
MASSAGE
SAVINGS
EXERCISE
SPIRITUAL WELL BEING
CREATIVITY
INVESTING
CARDIO
MUSIC
WEIGHT
MEDITATION
YOGA & STRETCHING
WALKING
DEEP BREATHING
TIME IN NATURE
CONTRIBUTING TO OTHERS

*My Weekly Reflection*

## What word best describes ME this week?

# My Authentic Heart Words

|  |  |  |  |  |  |
|---|---|---|---|---|---|
|  |  |  |  |  |  |

| Workout | Ⓐ Ⓒ | Ⓐ Ⓒ | Ⓐ Ⓒ | Ⓐ Ⓒ | Ⓐ Ⓒ | Ⓐ Ⓒ |
|---|---|---|---|---|---|---|
| Just for Me | ♥ | ♥ | ♥ | ♥ | ♥ | |
| Water | ⊔⊔⊔⊔⊔⊔ | ⊔⊔⊔⊔⊔⊔ | ⊔⊔⊔⊔⊔⊔ | ⊔⊔⊔⊔⊔⊔ | ⊔⊔⊔⊔⊔⊔ | ⊔⊔⊔⊔⊔⊔ |
| Wins ✓ | | | | | | |
| Daily Happy Moment ☺ | | | | | | |

| MONDAY ☐ | TUESDAY ☐ | WEDNESDAY ☐ | THURSDAY ☐ | FRIDAY ☐ | SATURDAY ☐ |
|---|---|---|---|---|---|
| 7:00 | 7:00 | 7:00 | 7:00 | 7:00 | |
| 8:00 | 8:00 | 8:00 | 8:00 | 8:00 | |
| 9:00 | 9:00 | 9:00 | 9:00 | 9:00 | |
| 10:00 | 10:00 | 10:00 | 10:00 | 10:00 | |
| 11:00 | 11:00 | 11:00 | 11:00 | 11:00 | |
| 12:00 | 12:00 | 12:00 | 12:00 | 12:00 | |
| 1:00 | 1:00 | 1:00 | 1:00 | 1:00 | |
| 2:00 | 2:00 | 2:00 | 2:00 | 2:00 | SUNDAY ☐ |
| 3:00 | 3:00 | 3:00 | 3:00 | 3:00 | |
| 4:00 | 4:00 | 4:00 | 4:00 | 4:00 | |
| 5:00 | 5:00 | 5:00 | 5:00 | 5:00 | |
| 6:00 | 6:00 | 6:00 | 6:00 | 6:00 | |
| 7:00 | 7:00 | 7:00 | 7:00 | 7:00 | |

| Do. Call | Do. Call | Do. Call | Do. Call | Do. Call | Do. Call |
|---|---|---|---|---|---|
|  |  |  |  |  |  |

| $ Money in | $ Money in | $ Money in | $ Money in | $ Money in | $ Money in |
|---|---|---|---|---|---|
|  |  |  |  |  |  |

## Remembering Me

I am: _____

What I love about me is: _____

_____

What I am proud of this week is: _____

_____

## Weekly Goals:

1. _____ ○    3. _____ ○

2. _____ ○    4. _____ ○

## Not to Miss:

· _____    · _____

· _____    · _____

## Projects to Complete:

_____

_____

_____

_____

## Recipes to Try:

_____

_____

_____

_____

## To Beautify my Home:

_____

_____

_____

_____

## Call - Email - Social Media:

· _____    · _____

· _____    · _____

· _____    · _____

· _____    · _____

## To Do:

_____    _____

_____    _____

_____    _____

## Groceries:

_____    _____

_____    _____

_____    _____

## To Buy:

· _____    · _____

· _____    · _____

· _____    · _____

## My Balanced Heart

KIND KIN DEED
FAMILY HOLIDAY
COUPLES DATES
FRIENDS
HAVING FUN TOGETHER
MY FAMILY
BESTIES
SPOUSES FAMILY
KIND KID DEED
KIDS & PETS
SPOUSE
ALONE TIME
GROWING
ME
SELF CARE
MASSAGE
READING
WORK
CREATIVITY
SAVINGS
EXERCISE
SPIRITUAL WELL BEING
MUSIC
INVESTING
MEDITATION
CARDIO
WEIGHT
DEEP BREATHING
YOGA & STRETCHING
WALKING
TIME IN NATURE
CONTRIBUTING TO OTHERS

## My Weekly Reflection

## What word best describes ME this week?

# My Authentic Heart Words

| | | | | | |
|---|---|---|---|---|---|
| | | | | | |

| Workout | Ⓐ Ⓒ | Ⓐ Ⓒ | Ⓐ Ⓒ | Ⓐ Ⓒ | Ⓐ Ⓒ | Ⓐ Ⓒ |
|---|---|---|---|---|---|---|
| Just for Me | ♥ | ♥ | ♥ | ♥ | ♥ | |
| Water | ⊔⊔⊔⊔⊔⊔⊔ | ⊔⊔⊔⊔⊔⊔⊔ | ⊔⊔⊔⊔⊔⊔⊔ | ⊔⊔⊔⊔⊔⊔⊔ | ⊔⊔⊔⊔⊔⊔⊔ | ⊔⊔⊔⊔⊔⊔⊔ |
| Wins ✓ | | | | | | |
| Daily Happy Moment ☺ | | | | | | |

| MONDAY ☐ | TUESDAY ☐ | WEDNESDAY ☐ | THURSDAY ☐ | FRIDAY ☐ | SATURDAY ☐ |
|---|---|---|---|---|---|
| 7:00 | 7:00 | 7:00 | 7:00 | 7:00 | |
| 8:00 | 8:00 | 8:00 | 8:00 | 8:00 | |
| 9:00 | 9:00 | 9:00 | 9:00 | 9:00 | |
| 10:00 | 10:00 | 10:00 | 10:00 | 10:00 | |
| 11:00 | 11:00 | 11:00 | 11:00 | 11:00 | |
| 12:00 | 12:00 | 12:00 | 12:00 | 12:00 | |
| 1:00 | 1:00 | 1:00 | 1:00 | 1:00 | |
| 2:00 | 2:00 | 2:00 | 2:00 | 2:00 | SUNDAY ☐ |
| 3:00 | 3:00 | 3:00 | 3:00 | 3:00 | |
| 4:00 | 4:00 | 4:00 | 4:00 | 4:00 | |
| 5:00 | 5:00 | 5:00 | 5:00 | 5:00 | |
| 6:00 | 6:00 | 6:00 | 6:00 | 6:00 | |
| 7:00 | 7:00 | 7:00 | 7:00 | 7:00 | |

| Do. Call | Do. Call | Do. Call | Do. Call | Do. Call | Do. Call |
|---|---|---|---|---|---|
| | | | | | |

| $ Money in | $ Money in | $ Money in | $ Money in | $ Money in | $ Money in |
|---|---|---|---|---|---|
| | | | | | |

## Remembering Me

I am: _____

What I love about me is: _____

_____

What I am proud of this week is: _____

_____

## Weekly Goals:

1. _____ ○   3. _____ ○

2. _____ ○   4. _____ ○

## Not to Miss:

· _____   · _____

· _____   · _____

## Projects to Complete:

_____

_____

_____

_____

## Recipes to Try:

_____

_____

_____

_____

## To Beautify my Home:

_____

_____

_____

_____

## Call - Email - Social Media:

· _____   · _____

· _____   · _____

· _____   · _____

· _____   · _____

## To Do:

_____   _____

_____   _____

_____   ## Groceries:

_____   _____   _____

_____   _____   _____

## To Buy:

· _____   · _____

· _____   · _____

· _____   · _____

_____   _____   _____

## My Balanced Heart

## My Weekly Reflection

## What word best describes ME this week?

81

# My Authentic Heart Words

| | | | | | |
|---|---|---|---|---|---|
| | | | | | |

| | | | | | | |
|---|---|---|---|---|---|---|
| Workout | Ⓐ Ⓒ | Ⓐ Ⓒ | Ⓐ Ⓒ | Ⓐ Ⓒ | Ⓐ Ⓒ | Ⓐ Ⓒ |
| Just for Me | ♥ | ♥ | ♥ | ♥ | ♥ | |
| Water | ⬜⬜⬜⬜⬜⬜ | ⬜⬜⬜⬜⬜⬜ | ⬜⬜⬜⬜⬜⬜ | ⬜⬜⬜⬜⬜⬜ | ⬜⬜⬜⬜⬜⬜ | ⬜⬜⬜⬜⬜⬜ |
| Wins ✓ | | | | | | |
| Daily Happy Moment ☺ | | | | | | |

| **MONDAY** ☐ | **TUESDAY** ☐ | **WEDNESDAY** ☐ | **THURSDAY** ☐ | **FRIDAY** ☐ | **SATURDAY** ☐ |
|---|---|---|---|---|---|
| 7:00 | 7:00 | 7:00 | 7:00 | 7:00 | |
| 8:00 | 8:00 | 8:00 | 8:00 | 8:00 | |
| 9:00 | 9:00 | 9:00 | 9:00 | 9:00 | |
| 10:00 | 10:00 | 10:00 | 10:00 | 10:00 | |
| 11:00 | 11:00 | 11:00 | 11:00 | 11:00 | |
| 12:00 | 12:00 | 12:00 | 12:00 | 12:00 | |
| 1:00 | 1:00 | 1:00 | 1:00 | 1:00 | |
| 2:00 | 2:00 | 2:00 | 2:00 | 2:00 | **SUNDAY** ☐ |
| 3:00 | 3:00 | 3:00 | 3:00 | 3:00 | |
| 4:00 | 4:00 | 4:00 | 4:00 | 4:00 | |
| 5:00 | 5:00 | 5:00 | 5:00 | 5:00 | |
| 6:00 | 6:00 | 6:00 | 6:00 | 6:00 | |
| 7:00 | 7:00 | 7:00 | 7:00 | 7:00 | |

| Do. Call | Do. Call | Do. Call | Do. Call | Do. Call | Do. Call |
|---|---|---|---|---|---|
| | | | | | |

| $ Money in | $ Money in | $ Money in | $ Money in | $ Money in | $ Money in |
|---|---|---|---|---|---|
| | | | | | |

## Remembering Me

I am: _____

What I love about me is: _____

_____

What I am proud of this week is: _____

_____

## Weekly Goals:

1. _____ ○    3. _____ ○

2. _____ ○    4. _____ ○

## Not to Miss:

· _____    · _____

· _____    · _____

## Projects to Complete:

_____
_____
_____
_____

## Recipes to Try:

_____
_____
_____
_____

## To Beautify my Home:

_____
_____
_____
_____

## Call - Email - Social Media:

· _____    · _____

· _____    · _____

· _____    · _____

· _____    · _____

## To Do:

_____
_____
_____
_____
_____

## Groceries:

_____ _____
_____ _____
_____ _____
_____ _____

## To Buy:

· _____    · _____

· _____    · _____

· _____    · _____

My Balanced Heart

COUPLES DATES
FRIENDS
HAVING FUN TOGETHER
SPOUSES FAMILY
ALONE TIME
MASSAGE
CREATIVITY
MUSIC
MEDITATION
DEEP BREATHING
TIME IN NATURE
CONTRIBUTING TO OTHERS
WALKING
YOGA & STRETCHING
WEIGHT
CARDIO
INVESTING
SAVINGS
READING
GROWING
KIND KID DEED
FAMILY HOLIDAY
KIND KIN DEED
MY FAMILY
BESTIES
SPOUSE
SELF CARE
ME
WORK
EXERCISE
SPIRITUAL WELL BEING
KIDS & PETS

My Weekly Reflection

What word best describes ME this week?

## This Month ♥

### Goals to Complete:
1. _____ ◯
2. _____ ◯
3. _____ ◯
4. _____ ◯
5. _____ ◯

### Places to Explore:
_____
_____
_____
_____

### To Buy:
·      ·
·      ·
·      ·

### Not to Miss:
·      ·
·      ·
·      ·

### Favorite Books I am Reading:
·      ·
·      ·

# Month: _____

| SUNDAY | MONDAY | TUESDAY |
|--------|--------|---------|
|  |  |  |
|  |  |  |
|  |  |  |
|  |  |  |
|  |  |  |

## ♥ PLAN OF ACTION

| Work: | Personal: | Misc: |
|-------|-----------|-------|
| ◯ _____ | ◯ _____ | ◯ _____ |
| ◯ _____ | ◯ _____ | ◯ _____ |
| ◯ _____ | ◯ _____ | ◯ _____ |
| ◯ _____ | ◯ _____ | ◯ _____ |
| ◯ _____ | ◯ _____ | ◯ _____ |
| ◯ _____ | ◯ _____ | ◯ _____ |
| ◯ _____ | ◯ _____ | ◯ _____ |
| ◯ _____ | ◯ _____ | ◯ _____ |

*"Find your happy, sooner than later."* ~ Unknown

| WEDNESDAY | THURSDAY | FRIDAY | SATURDAY |
|---|---|---|---|
| | | | |
| | | | |
| | | | |
| | | | |
| | | | |

### What made my ♥ happy this month...

_____
_____
_____
_____
_____
_____
_____

With gratitude & love, thank you.

## My Accomplishments this Month

### Improvements In My Life:
.
.
.
.

### Good Deeds Done:
.
.
.
.

### Fun and Spontaneous:
.
.
.

### I Treated Myself To:
.
.
.
.

### New Experiences:
.
.
.
.

### My Manifestation List:
| CLAIM AS TRUE | DATE RECEIVED |
|---|---|
| 1. _____ | _____ |
| 2. _____ | _____ |
| 3. _____ | _____ |
| 4. _____ | _____ |
| 5. _____ | _____ |

# $ Keeping Track of the Flow of it All

Month: _____

| DATES + DETAILS | MONEY IN | SAVINGS | SHARING WITH OTHERS | INSURANCE + HEALTH EXPENSES | HOUSE EXPENSES | GROCERIES | TRANSPORTATION EXPENSES | ENTERTAINMENT + FUN EXPENSES | HOLIDAY EXPENSES | PERSONAL EXPENSES | DINING OUT | MISC |
|---|---|---|---|---|---|---|---|---|---|---|---|---|
| | | | | | | | | | | | | |
| | | | | | | | | | | | | |
| | | | | | | | | | | | | |
| | | | | | | | | | | | | |
| | | | | | | | | | | | | |
| | | | | | | | | | | | | |
| | | | | | | | | | | | | |
| | | | | | | | | | | | | |
| | | | | | | | | | | | | |
| | | | | | | | | | | | | |
| | | | | | | | | | | | | |
| | | | | | | | | | | | | |
| | | | | | | | | | | | | |
| | | | | | | | | | | | | |
| | | | | | | | | | | | | |
| $ TOTALS | | | | | | | | | | | | |

# My Journaling Space ♥

# My Authentic Heart Words

|  |  |  |  |  |  |
|---|---|---|---|---|---|
|  |  |  |  |  |  |

| | | | | | | |
|---|---|---|---|---|---|---|
| Workout | Ⓐ Ⓒ | Ⓐ Ⓒ | Ⓐ Ⓒ | Ⓐ Ⓒ | Ⓐ Ⓒ | Ⓐ Ⓒ |
| Just for Me | ♥ | ♥ | ♥ | ♥ | ♥ | |
| Water | □□□□□□ | □□□□□□ | □□□□□□ | □□□□□□ | □□□□□□ | □□□□□□ |
| Wins ✓ | | | | | | |
| Daily Happy Moment ☺ | | | | | | |

| MONDAY ☐ | TUESDAY ☐ | WEDNESDAY ☐ | THURSDAY ☐ | FRIDAY ☐ | SATURDAY ☐ |
|---|---|---|---|---|---|
| 7:00 | 7:00 | 7:00 | 7:00 | 7:00 | |
| 8:00 | 8:00 | 8:00 | 8:00 | 8:00 | |
| 9:00 | 9:00 | 9:00 | 9:00 | 9:00 | |
| 10:00 | 10:00 | 10:00 | 10:00 | 10:00 | |
| 11:00 | 11:00 | 11:00 | 11:00 | 11:00 | |
| 12:00 | 12:00 | 12:00 | 12:00 | 12:00 | |
| 1:00 | 1:00 | 1:00 | 1:00 | 1:00 | |
| 2:00 | 2:00 | 2:00 | 2:00 | 2:00 | SUNDAY ☐ |
| 3:00 | 3:00 | 3:00 | 3:00 | 3:00 | |
| 4:00 | 4:00 | 4:00 | 4:00 | 4:00 | |
| 5:00 | 5:00 | 5:00 | 5:00 | 5:00 | |
| 6:00 | 6:00 | 6:00 | 6:00 | 6:00 | |
| 7:00 | 7:00 | 7:00 | 7:00 | 7:00 | |

| Do. Call | Do. Call | Do. Call | Do. Call | Do. Call | Do. Call |
|---|---|---|---|---|---|
| | | | | | |

| $ Money in | $ Money in | $ Money in | $ Money in | $ Money in | $ Money in |
|---|---|---|---|---|---|
| | | | | | |

## Remembering Me

I am: _____

What I love about me is: _____

_____

What I am proud of this week is: _____

_____

## Weekly Goals:

1. _____ ○   3. _____ ○

2. _____ ○   4. _____ ○

## Not to Miss:

· _____   · _____

· _____   · _____

## Projects to Complete:

_____

_____

_____

_____

## Recipes to Try:

_____

_____

_____

_____

## To Beautify my Home:

_____

_____

_____

_____

## Call - Email - Social Media:

· _____   · _____

· _____   · _____

· _____   · _____

· _____   · _____

## To Buy:

· _____   · _____

· _____   · _____

· _____   · _____

## To Do:

_____   _____

_____   _____

_____   _____

### Groceries:

_____   _____

_____   _____

_____   _____

_____   _____

## My Balanced Heart

COUPLES DATES, FRIENDS, HAVING FUN TOGETHER, SPOUSES FAMILY, SPOUSE, ALONE TIME, MASSAGE, CREATIVITY, MUSIC, MEDITATION, DEEP BREATHING, TIME IN NATURE, CONTRIBUTING TO OTHERS, WALKING, YOGA & STRETCHING, WEIGHT, CARDIO, INVESTING, SAVINGS, READING, GROWING, KIND KID DEED, FAMILY HOLIDAY, KIND KIN DEED

MY FAMILY, BESTIES, KIDS & PETS, SPOUSE, WORK, SELF CARE, EXERCISE, SPIRITUAL WELL BEING, ME

## My Weekly Reflection

## What word best describes ME this week?

89

# My Authentic Heart Words

|  |  |  |  |  |  |
|---|---|---|---|---|---|
|  |  |  |  |  |  |

| Workout | Ⓐ Ⓒ | Ⓐ Ⓒ | Ⓐ Ⓒ | Ⓐ Ⓒ | Ⓐ Ⓒ | Ⓐ Ⓒ |
|---|---|---|---|---|---|---|
| Just for Me | ♥ | ♥ | ♥ | ♥ | ♥ | |
| Water | ⬜⬜⬜⬜⬜⬜ | ⬜⬜⬜⬜⬜⬜ | ⬜⬜⬜⬜⬜⬜ | ⬜⬜⬜⬜⬜⬜ | ⬜⬜⬜⬜⬜⬜ | ⬜⬜⬜⬜⬜⬜ |
| Wins ✓ | | | | | | |
| Daily Happy Moment ☺ | | | | | | |

## MONDAY ☐

7:00
8:00
9:00
10:00
11:00
12:00
1:00
2:00
3:00
4:00
5:00
6:00
7:00

### Do. Call

### $ Money in

## TUESDAY ☐

7:00
8:00
9:00
10:00
11:00
12:00
1:00
2:00
3:00
4:00
5:00
6:00
7:00

### Do. Call

### $ Money in

## WEDNESDAY ☐

7:00
8:00
9:00
10:00
11:00
12:00
1:00
2:00
3:00
4:00
5:00
6:00
7:00

### Do. Call

### $ Money in

## THURSDAY ☐

7:00
8:00
9:00
10:00
11:00
12:00
1:00
2:00
3:00
4:00
5:00
6:00
7:00

### Do. Call

### $ Money in

## FRIDAY ☐

7:00
8:00
9:00
10:00
11:00
12:00
1:00
2:00
3:00
4:00
5:00
6:00
7:00

### Do. Call

### $ Money in

## SATURDAY ☐

## SUNDAY ☐

### Do. Call

### $ Money in

## Remembering Me

I am: _____

What I love about me is: _____

_____

What I am proud of this week is: _____

_____

## Weekly Goals:

1. _____ ○   3. _____ ○

2. _____ ○   4. _____ ○

## Not to Miss:

- 
- 

- 
- 

## Projects to Complete:

_____

_____

_____

_____

## Recipes to Try:

_____

_____

_____

_____

## To Beautify my Home:

_____

_____

_____

_____

## Call - Email - Social Media:

- 
- 
- 
- 

- 
- 
- 
- 

## To Buy:

- 
- 
- 

- 
- 
- 

## To Do:

_____  _____

_____  _____

_____

### Groceries:

_____  _____  _____

_____  _____  _____

_____  _____  _____

*My Balanced Heart*

*My Weekly Reflection*

## What word best describes ME this week?

# My Authentic Heart Words

| | | | | | |
|---|---|---|---|---|---|
| | | | | | |

| Workout | Ⓐ Ⓒ | Ⓐ Ⓒ | Ⓐ Ⓒ | Ⓐ Ⓒ | Ⓐ Ⓒ | Ⓐ Ⓒ |
|---|---|---|---|---|---|---|
| Just for Me | ♥ | ♥ | ♥ | ♥ | ♥ | |
| Water | ▽▽▽▽▽▽▽ | ▽▽▽▽▽▽▽ | ▽▽▽▽▽▽▽ | ▽▽▽▽▽▽▽ | ▽▽▽▽▽▽▽ | ▽▽▽▽▽▽▽ |
| Wins ✓ | | | | | | |
| Daily Happy Moment ☺ | | | | | | |

| MONDAY ☐ | TUESDAY ☐ | WEDNESDAY ☐ | THURSDAY ☐ | FRIDAY ☐ | SATURDAY ☐ |
|---|---|---|---|---|---|
| 7:00 | 7:00 | 7:00 | 7:00 | 7:00 | |
| 8:00 | 8:00 | 8:00 | 8:00 | 8:00 | |
| 9:00 | 9:00 | 9:00 | 9:00 | 9:00 | |
| 10:00 | 10:00 | 10:00 | 10:00 | 10:00 | |
| 11:00 | 11:00 | 11:00 | 11:00 | 11:00 | |
| 12:00 | 12:00 | 12:00 | 12:00 | 12:00 | |
| 1:00 | 1:00 | 1:00 | 1:00 | 1:00 | |
| 2:00 | 2:00 | 2:00 | 2:00 | 2:00 | SUNDAY ☐ |
| 3:00 | 3:00 | 3:00 | 3:00 | 3:00 | |
| 4:00 | 4:00 | 4:00 | 4:00 | 4:00 | |
| 5:00 | 5:00 | 5:00 | 5:00 | 5:00 | |
| 6:00 | 6:00 | 6:00 | 6:00 | 6:00 | |
| 7:00 | 7:00 | 7:00 | 7:00 | 7:00 | |

| Do. Call | Do. Call | Do. Call | Do. Call | Do. Call | Do. Call |
|---|---|---|---|---|---|
| | | | | | |

| $ Money in | $ Money in | $ Money in | $ Money in | $ Money in | $ Money in |
|---|---|---|---|---|---|
| | | | | | |

## Remembering Me

I am: _____

What I love about me is: _____

_____

What I am proud of this week is: _____

_____

## Weekly Goals:

1. _____ ◯  3. _____ ◯

2. _____ ◯  4. _____ ◯

## Not to Miss:

- _____    - _____

- _____    - _____

## Projects to Complete:

_____
_____
_____
_____

## Recipes to Try:

_____
_____
_____
_____

## To Beautify my Home:

_____
_____
_____
_____

## Call - Email - Social Media:

- _____    - _____
- _____    - _____
- _____    - _____
- _____    - _____

## To Buy:

- _____    - _____
- _____    - _____
- _____    - _____

## To Do:

_____    _____
_____    _____
_____

## Groceries:

_____    _____
_____    _____
_____    _____

My Balanced Heart

FAMILY HOLIDAY · KIND KIN DEED · COUPLES DATES · FRIENDS · HAVING FUN TOGETHER · KIND KID DEED · MY FAMILY · BESTIES · SPOUSES FAMILY · KIDS & PETS · SPOUSE · GROWING · ME · SELF CARE · ALONE TIME · READING · WORK · MASSAGE · SAVINGS · EXERCISE · CREATIVITY · INVESTING · SPIRITUAL WELL BEING · MUSIC · CARDIO · MEDITATION · WEIGHT · YOGA & STRETCHING · WALKING · DEEP BREATHING · TIME IN NATURE · CONTRIBUTING TO OTHERS

## My Weekly Reflection

## What word best describes ME this week?

# My Authentic Heart Words

|  | | | | | |
|---|---|---|---|---|---|
| | | | | | |

| | | | | | | |
|---|---|---|---|---|---|---|
| Workout | Ⓐ Ⓒ | Ⓐ Ⓒ | Ⓐ Ⓒ | Ⓐ Ⓒ | Ⓐ Ⓒ | Ⓐ Ⓒ |
| Just for Me | ♥ | ♥ | ♥ | ♥ | ♥ | |
| Water | ⬜⬜⬜⬜⬜⬜ | ⬜⬜⬜⬜⬜⬜ | ⬜⬜⬜⬜⬜⬜ | ⬜⬜⬜⬜⬜⬜ | ⬜⬜⬜⬜⬜⬜ | ⬜⬜⬜⬜⬜⬜ |
| Wins ✓ | | | | | | |
| Daily Happy Moment ☺ | | | | | | |

| MONDAY ☐ | TUESDAY ☐ | WEDNESDAY ☐ | THURSDAY ☐ | FRIDAY ☐ | SATURDAY ☐ |
|---|---|---|---|---|---|
| 7:00 | 7:00 | 7:00 | 7:00 | 7:00 | |
| 8:00 | 8:00 | 8:00 | 8:00 | 8:00 | |
| 9:00 | 9:00 | 9:00 | 9:00 | 9:00 | |
| 10:00 | 10:00 | 10:00 | 10:00 | 10:00 | |
| 11:00 | 11:00 | 11:00 | 11:00 | 11:00 | |
| 12:00 | 12:00 | 12:00 | 12:00 | 12:00 | |
| 1:00 | 1:00 | 1:00 | 1:00 | 1:00 | |
| 2:00 | 2:00 | 2:00 | 2:00 | 2:00 | SUNDAY ☐ |
| 3:00 | 3:00 | 3:00 | 3:00 | 3:00 | |
| 4:00 | 4:00 | 4:00 | 4:00 | 4:00 | |
| 5:00 | 5:00 | 5:00 | 5:00 | 5:00 | |
| 6:00 | 6:00 | 6:00 | 6:00 | 6:00 | |
| 7:00 | 7:00 | 7:00 | 7:00 | 7:00 | |

| Do. Call | Do. Call | Do. Call | Do. Call | Do. Call | Do. Call |
|---|---|---|---|---|---|
| | | | | | |

| $ Money in | $ Money in | $ Money in | $ Money in | $ Money in | $ Money in |
|---|---|---|---|---|---|
| | | | | | |

## Remembering Me

I am: _____

What I love about me is: _____

_____

What I am proud of this week is: _____

_____

## Weekly Goals:

1. _____ ○     3. _____ ○

2. _____ ○     4. _____ ○

## Not to Miss:

· _____     · _____

· _____     · _____

## Projects to Complete:

_____

_____

_____

_____

## Recipes to Try:

_____

_____

_____

_____

## To Beautify my Home:

_____

_____

_____

_____

## Call - Email - Social Media:

· _____     · _____

· _____     · _____

· _____     · _____

· _____     · _____

## To Do:

_____     _____

_____     _____

_____

## Groceries:

_____     _____

_____     _____

_____     _____

_____     _____

_____     _____

## To Buy:

· _____     · _____

· _____     · _____

· _____     · _____

## My Balanced Heart

FAMILY HOLIDAY · KIND KIN DEED · COUPLES DATES · FRIENDS · HAVING FUN TOGETHER · MY FAMILY · BESTIES · SPOUSES FAMILY · KIND KID DEED · KIDS & PETS · SPOUSE · ALONE TIME · GROWING · WORK · ME · SELF CARE · MASSAGE · READING · EXERCISE · SPIRITUAL WELL BEING · CREATIVITY · SAVINGS · MUSIC · INVESTING · CARDIO · MEDITATION · WEIGHT · DEEP BREATHING · YOGA & STRETCHING · WALKING · TIME IN NATURE · CONTRIBUTING TO OTHERS

## My Weekly Reflection

## What word best describes ME this week?

# My Authentic Heart Words

|  |  |  |  |  |  |
|---|---|---|---|---|---|
| | | | | | |

| | | | | | | |
|---|---|---|---|---|---|---|
| Workout | Ⓐ Ⓒ | Ⓐ Ⓒ | Ⓐ Ⓒ | Ⓐ Ⓒ | Ⓐ Ⓒ | Ⓐ Ⓒ |
| Just for Me | ♥ | ♥ | ♥ | ♥ | ♥ | |
| Water | ⊔⊔⊔⊔⊔⊔⊔ | ⊔⊔⊔⊔⊔⊔⊔ | ⊔⊔⊔⊔⊔⊔⊔ | ⊔⊔⊔⊔⊔⊔⊔ | ⊔⊔⊔⊔⊔⊔⊔ | ⊔⊔⊔⊔⊔⊔⊔ |
| Wins ✓ | | | | | | |
| Daily Happy Moment ☺ | | | | | | |

| MONDAY ☐ | TUESDAY ☐ | WEDNESDAY ☐ | THURSDAY ☐ | FRIDAY ☐ | SATURDAY ☐ |
|---|---|---|---|---|---|
| 7:00 | 7:00 | 7:00 | 7:00 | 7:00 | |
| 8:00 | 8:00 | 8:00 | 8:00 | 8:00 | |
| 9:00 | 9:00 | 9:00 | 9:00 | 9:00 | |
| 10:00 | 10:00 | 10:00 | 10:00 | 10:00 | |
| 11:00 | 11:00 | 11:00 | 11:00 | 11:00 | |
| 12:00 | 12:00 | 12:00 | 12:00 | 12:00 | |
| 1:00 | 1:00 | 1:00 | 1:00 | 1:00 | |
| 2:00 | 2:00 | 2:00 | 2:00 | 2:00 | SUNDAY ☐ |
| 3:00 | 3:00 | 3:00 | 3:00 | 3:00 | |
| 4:00 | 4:00 | 4:00 | 4:00 | 4:00 | |
| 5:00 | 5:00 | 5:00 | 5:00 | 5:00 | |
| 6:00 | 6:00 | 6:00 | 6:00 | 6:00 | |
| 7:00 | 7:00 | 7:00 | 7:00 | 7:00 | |

| Do. Call | Do. Call | Do. Call | Do. Call | Do. Call | Do. Call |
|---|---|---|---|---|---|
| | | | | | |

| $ Money in | $ Money in | $ Money in | $ Money in | $ Money in | $ Money in |
|---|---|---|---|---|---|
| | | | | | |

## Remembering Me

I am: _____

What I love about me is: _____

_____

What I am proud of this week is: _____

_____

## Weekly Goals:

1. _____ ○     3. _____ ○

2. _____ ○     4. _____ ○

## Not to Miss:

· _____     · _____

· _____     · _____

## Projects to Complete:

_____

_____

_____

_____

## Recipes to Try:

_____

_____

_____

_____

## To Beautify my Home:

_____

_____

_____

_____

## Call - Email - Social Media:

· _____     · _____

· _____     · _____

· _____     · _____

· _____     · _____

## To Do:

_____

_____

_____

## Groceries:

_____

_____

_____

## To Buy:

· _____     · _____

· _____     · _____

· _____     · _____

## My Balanced Heart

COUPLES DATES
FRIENDS
HAVING FUN TOGETHER
SPOUSES FAMILY
ALONE TIME
MASSAGE
CREATIVITY
MUSIC
MEDITATION
DEEP BREATHING
TIME IN NATURE
CONTRIBUTING TO OTHERS
WALKING
YOGA & STRETCHING
WEIGHT
CARDIO
INVESTING
SAVINGS
READING
GROWING
KIND KID DEED
FAMILY HOLIDAY
KIND KIN DEED
MY FAMILY
BESTIES
SPOUSE
SELF CARE
SPIRITUAL WELL BEING
EXERCISE
WORK
KIDS & PETS
ME

## My Weekly Reflection

## What word best describes ME this week?

**This Month ♥**

## Goals to Complete:

1. _____ ○
2. _____ ○
3. _____ ○
4. _____ ○
5. _____ ○

## Places to Explore:

_____
_____
_____
_____
_____

## To Buy:

· ·
· ·
· ·

## Not to Miss:

· ·
· ·
· ·

## Favorite Books I am Reading:

· ·
· ·

# Month: _____

| SUNDAY | MONDAY | TUESDAY |
|--------|--------|---------|
|        |        |         |
|        |        |         |
|        |        |         |
|        |        |         |
|        |        |         |

## ♥ PLAN OF ACTION

| Work: | Personal: | Misc: |
|-------|-----------|-------|
| ○ _____ | ○ _____ | ○ _____ |
| ○ _____ | ○ _____ | ○ _____ |
| ○ _____ | ○ _____ | ○ _____ |
| ○ _____ | ○ _____ | ○ _____ |
| ○ _____ | ○ _____ | ○ _____ |
| ○ _____ | ○ _____ | ○ _____ |
| ○ _____ | ○ _____ | ○ _____ |
| ○ _____ | ○ _____ | ○ _____ |

*"The best way to predict the future is to create it."* ~ Unknown

| WEDNESDAY | THURSDAY | FRIDAY | SATURDAY |
|---|---|---|---|
|  |  |  |  |
|  |  |  |  |
|  |  |  |  |
|  |  |  |  |
|  |  |  |  |

### What made my ♥ happy this month...

_____
_____
_____
_____
_____
_____
_____
_____

With gratitude & love, thank you.

## My Accomplishments this Month

### Improvements In My Life:
.
.
.
.

### Good Deeds Done:
.
.
.
.

### Fun and Spontaneous:
.
.
.
.

### I Treated Myself To:
.
.
.
.

### New Experiences:
.
.
.
.

### My Manifestation List:

| | CLAIM AS TRUE | DATE RECEIVED |
|---|---|---|
| 1. | _____ | _____ |
| 2. | _____ | _____ |
| 3. | _____ | _____ |
| 4. | _____ | _____ |
| 5. | _____ | _____ |

# $ Keeping Track of the Flow of it All

**Month:** _____

| DATES + DETAILS | MONEY IN | SAVINGS | SHARING WITH OTHERS | INSURANCE + HEALTH EXPENSES | HOUSE EXPENSES | GROCERIES | TRANSPORTATION EXPENSES | ENTERTAINMENT + FUN EXPENSES | HOLIDAY EXPENSES | PERSONAL EXPENSES | DINING OUT | MISC |
|---|---|---|---|---|---|---|---|---|---|---|---|---|
| | | | | | | | | | | | | |
| | | | | | | | | | | | | |
| | | | | | | | | | | | | |
| | | | | | | | | | | | | |
| | | | | | | | | | | | | |
| | | | | | | | | | | | | |
| | | | | | | | | | | | | |
| | | | | | | | | | | | | |
| | | | | | | | | | | | | |
| | | | | | | | | | | | | |
| | | | | | | | | | | | | |
| | | | | | | | | | | | | |
| | | | | | | | | | | | | |
| | | | | | | | | | | | | |
| | | | | | | | | | | | | |
| | | | | | | | | | | | | |
| | | | | | | | | | | | | |
| $ TOTALS | | | | | | | | | | | | |

# My Journaling Space ♥

## My Authentic Heart Words

|  | | | | | |
|---|---|---|---|---|---|
| | | | | | |

| | | | | | | |
|---|---|---|---|---|---|---|
| Workout | Ⓐ Ⓒ | Ⓐ Ⓒ | Ⓐ Ⓒ | Ⓐ Ⓒ | Ⓐ Ⓒ | Ⓐ Ⓒ |
| Just for Me | ♥ | ♥ | ♥ | ♥ | ♥ | |
| Water | ▭▭▭▭▭▭ | ▭▭▭▭▭▭ | ▭▭▭▭▭▭ | ▭▭▭▭▭▭ | ▭▭▭▭▭▭ | ▭▭▭▭▭▭ |
| Wins ✓ | | | | | | |
| Daily Happy Moment ☺ | | | | | | |

| MONDAY ☐ | TUESDAY ☐ | WEDNESDAY ☐ | THURSDAY ☐ | FRIDAY ☐ | SATURDAY ☐ |
|---|---|---|---|---|---|
| 7:00 | 7:00 | 7:00 | 7:00 | 7:00 | |
| 8:00 | 8:00 | 8:00 | 8:00 | 8:00 | |
| 9:00 | 9:00 | 9:00 | 9:00 | 9:00 | |
| 10:00 | 10:00 | 10:00 | 10:00 | 10:00 | |
| 11:00 | 11:00 | 11:00 | 11:00 | 11:00 | |
| 12:00 | 12:00 | 12:00 | 12:00 | 12:00 | |
| 1:00 | 1:00 | 1:00 | 1:00 | 1:00 | |
| 2:00 | 2:00 | 2:00 | 2:00 | 2:00 | SUNDAY ☐ |
| 3:00 | 3:00 | 3:00 | 3:00 | 3:00 | |
| 4:00 | 4:00 | 4:00 | 4:00 | 4:00 | |
| 5:00 | 5:00 | 5:00 | 5:00 | 5:00 | |
| 6:00 | 6:00 | 6:00 | 6:00 | 6:00 | |
| 7:00 | 7:00 | 7:00 | 7:00 | 7:00 | |

| Do. Call | Do. Call | Do. Call | Do. Call | Do. Call | Do. Call |
|---|---|---|---|---|---|
| | | | | | |

| $ Money in | $ Money in | $ Money in | $ Money in | $ Money in | $ Money in |
|---|---|---|---|---|---|
| | | | | | |

## Remembering Me

I am: _____

What I love about me is: _____

_____

What I am proud of this week is: _____

_____

## Weekly Goals:

1. _____ ○    3. _____ ○

2. _____ ○    4. _____ ○

## Not to Miss:

- .                        .
- .                        .

## Projects to Complete:

_____

_____

_____

_____

## Recipes to Try:

_____

_____

_____

_____

## To Beautify my Home:

_____

_____

_____

_____

## Call - Email - Social Media:

- .                        .
- .                        .
- .                        .
- .                        .

## To Do:

_____

_____

_____

_____

_____

_____

### Groceries:

_____    _____

_____    _____

_____    _____

## To Buy:

- .                        .
- .                        .
- .                        .

*My Balanced Heart*

COUPLES DATES
FRIENDS
HAVING FUN TOGETHER
SPOUSES FAMILY
ALONE TIME
MASSAGE
CREATIVITY
MUSIC
MEDITATION
DEEP BREATHING
TIME IN NATURE
CONTRIBUTING TO OTHERS
WALKING
YOGA & STRETCHING
WEIGHT
CARDIO
INVESTING
SAVINGS
READING
GROWING
KIND KID DEED
FAMILY HOLIDAY
KIND KIN DEED
MY FAMILY
BESTIES
KIDS & PETS
SPOUSE
ME
SELF CARE
WORK
EXERCISE
SPIRITUAL WELL BEING

*My Weekly Reflection*

## What word best describes ME this week?

# My Authentic Heart Words

| | | | | | |
|---|---|---|---|---|---|
| | | | | | |

| | | | | | | |
|---|---|---|---|---|---|---|
| Workout | Ⓐ Ⓒ | Ⓐ Ⓒ | Ⓐ Ⓒ | Ⓐ Ⓒ | Ⓐ Ⓒ | Ⓐ Ⓒ |
| Just for Me | ♥ | ♥ | ♥ | ♥ | ♥ | |
| Water | ⬜⬜⬜⬜⬜⬜⬜ | ⬜⬜⬜⬜⬜⬜⬜ | ⬜⬜⬜⬜⬜⬜⬜ | ⬜⬜⬜⬜⬜⬜⬜ | ⬜⬜⬜⬜⬜⬜⬜ | ⬜⬜⬜⬜⬜⬜⬜ |
| Wins ✓ | | | | | | |
| Daily Happy Moment ☺ | | | | | | |

| MONDAY ☐ | TUESDAY ☐ | WEDNESDAY ☐ | THURSDAY ☐ | FRIDAY ☐ | SATURDAY ☐ |
|---|---|---|---|---|---|
| 7:00 | 7:00 | 7:00 | 7:00 | 7:00 | |
| 8:00 | 8:00 | 8:00 | 8:00 | 8:00 | |
| 9:00 | 9:00 | 9:00 | 9:00 | 9:00 | |
| 10:00 | 10:00 | 10:00 | 10:00 | 10:00 | |
| 11:00 | 11:00 | 11:00 | 11:00 | 11:00 | |
| 12:00 | 12:00 | 12:00 | 12:00 | 12:00 | |
| 1:00 | 1:00 | 1:00 | 1:00 | 1:00 | |
| 2:00 | 2:00 | 2:00 | 2:00 | 2:00 | SUNDAY ☐ |
| 3:00 | 3:00 | 3:00 | 3:00 | 3:00 | |
| 4:00 | 4:00 | 4:00 | 4:00 | 4:00 | |
| 5:00 | 5:00 | 5:00 | 5:00 | 5:00 | |
| 6:00 | 6:00 | 6:00 | 6:00 | 6:00 | |
| 7:00 | 7:00 | 7:00 | 7:00 | 7:00 | |

| Do. Call | Do. Call | Do. Call | Do. Call | Do. Call | Do. Call |
|---|---|---|---|---|---|
| | | | | | |

| $ Money in | $ Money in | $ Money in | $ Money in | $ Money in | $ Money in |
|---|---|---|---|---|---|
| | | | | | |

## Remembering Me

I am: _____

What I love about me is: _____

_____

What I am proud of this week is: _____

_____

## Weekly Goals:

1. _____ ○   3. _____ ○

2. _____ ○   4. _____ ○

## Not to Miss:

· _____     · _____

· _____     · _____

## Projects to Complete:

_____

_____

_____

_____

## Recipes to Try:

_____

_____

_____

_____

## To Beautify my Home:

_____

_____

_____

_____

## Call - Email - Social Media:

· _____     · _____

· _____     · _____

· _____     · _____

· _____     · _____

## To Do:

_____     _____

_____     _____

_____     

## Groceries:

_____     _____

## To Buy:

· _____     · _____

· _____     · _____

· _____     · _____

_____     _____

_____     _____

_____     _____

_____     _____

My Balanced Heart

## My Weekly Reflection

## What word best describes ME this week?

# My Authentic Heart Words

| | | | | | |
|---|---|---|---|---|---|
| | | | | | |

| | | | | | | |
|---|---|---|---|---|---|---|
| Workout | Ⓐ Ⓒ | Ⓐ Ⓒ | Ⓐ Ⓒ | Ⓐ Ⓒ | Ⓐ Ⓒ | Ⓐ Ⓒ |
| Just for Me | ♥ | ♥ | ♥ | ♥ | ♥ | |
| Water | ⊔⊔⊔⊔⊔⊔⊔ | ⊔⊔⊔⊔⊔⊔⊔ | ⊔⊔⊔⊔⊔⊔⊔ | ⊔⊔⊔⊔⊔⊔⊔ | ⊔⊔⊔⊔⊔⊔⊔ | ⊔⊔⊔⊔⊔⊔⊔ |
| Wins ✓ | | | | | | |
| Daily Happy Moment ☺ | | | | | | |

| MONDAY ☐ | TUESDAY ☐ | WEDNESDAY ☐ | THURSDAY ☐ | FRIDAY ☐ | SATURDAY ☐ |
|---|---|---|---|---|---|
| 7:00 | 7:00 | 7:00 | 7:00 | 7:00 | |
| 8:00 | 8:00 | 8:00 | 8:00 | 8:00 | |
| 9:00 | 9:00 | 9:00 | 9:00 | 9:00 | |
| 10:00 | 10:00 | 10:00 | 10:00 | 10:00 | |
| 11:00 | 11:00 | 11:00 | 11:00 | 11:00 | |
| 12:00 | 12:00 | 12:00 | 12:00 | 12:00 | |
| 1:00 | 1:00 | 1:00 | 1:00 | 1:00 | |
| 2:00 | 2:00 | 2:00 | 2:00 | 2:00 | SUNDAY ☐ |
| 3:00 | 3:00 | 3:00 | 3:00 | 3:00 | |
| 4:00 | 4:00 | 4:00 | 4:00 | 4:00 | |
| 5:00 | 5:00 | 5:00 | 5:00 | 5:00 | |
| 6:00 | 6:00 | 6:00 | 6:00 | 6:00 | |
| 7:00 | 7:00 | 7:00 | 7:00 | 7:00 | |

| Do. Call | Do. Call | Do. Call | Do. Call | Do. Call | Do. Call |
|---|---|---|---|---|---|
| | | | | | |

| $ Money in | $ Money in | $ Money in | $ Money in | $ Money in | $ Money in |
|---|---|---|---|---|---|
| | | | | | |

## Remembering Me

I am: _____

What I love about me is: _____

_____

What I am proud of this week is: _____

_____

## Weekly Goals:

1. _____ ◯    3. _____ ◯

2. _____ ◯    4. _____ ◯

## Not to Miss:

·

·

·

·

## Projects to Complete:

_____

_____

_____

## Recipes to Try:

_____

_____

_____

## To Beautify my Home:

_____

_____

_____

## Call - Email - Social Media:

·        ·

·        ·

·        ·

·        ·

## To Do:

_____

_____

_____

## Groceries:

_____

_____

_____

_____

## To Buy:

·

·

·

### My Balanced Heart

KIND KIN DEED
FAMILY HOLIDAY
COUPLES DATES
FRIENDS
HAVING FUN TOGETHER
KIND KID DEED
MY FAMILY
BESTIES
SPOUSES FAMILY
GROWING
KIDS & PETS
SPOUSE
ALONE TIME
READING
ME
SELF CARE
MASSAGE
WORK
SAVINGS
CREATIVITY
INVESTING
EXERCISE
SPIRITUAL WELL BEING
MUSIC
CARDIO
MEDITATION
WEIGHT
DEEP BREATHING
YOGA & STRETCHING
WALKING
TIME IN NATURE
CONTRIBUTING TO OTHERS

### My Weekly Reflection

### What word best describes ME this week?

# My Authentic Heart Words

| | | | | | |
|---|---|---|---|---|---|
| | | | | | |

| Workout | Ⓐ Ⓒ | Ⓐ Ⓒ | Ⓐ Ⓒ | Ⓐ Ⓒ | Ⓐ Ⓒ | Ⓐ Ⓒ |

| Just for Me | ♥ | ♥ | ♥ | ♥ | ♥ | |

**Water**

| | | | | | |
|---|---|---|---|---|---|
| ☐☐☐☐☐☐☐ | ☐☐☐☐☐☐☐ | ☐☐☐☐☐☐☐ | ☐☐☐☐☐☐☐ | ☐☐☐☐☐☐☐ | ☐☐☐☐☐☐☐ |

**Wins ✓**

**Daily Happy Moment ☺**

| MONDAY ☐ | TUESDAY ☐ | WEDNESDAY ☐ | THURSDAY ☐ | FRIDAY ☐ | SATURDAY ☐ |
|---|---|---|---|---|---|
| 7:00 | 7:00 | 7:00 | 7:00 | 7:00 | |
| 8:00 | 8:00 | 8:00 | 8:00 | 8:00 | |
| 9:00 | 9:00 | 9:00 | 9:00 | 9:00 | |
| 10:00 | 10:00 | 10:00 | 10:00 | 10:00 | |
| 11:00 | 11:00 | 11:00 | 11:00 | 11:00 | |
| 12:00 | 12:00 | 12:00 | 12:00 | 12:00 | |
| 1:00 | 1:00 | 1:00 | 1:00 | 1:00 | |
| 2:00 | 2:00 | 2:00 | 2:00 | 2:00 | **SUNDAY** ☐ |
| 3:00 | 3:00 | 3:00 | 3:00 | 3:00 | |
| 4:00 | 4:00 | 4:00 | 4:00 | 4:00 | |
| 5:00 | 5:00 | 5:00 | 5:00 | 5:00 | |
| 6:00 | 6:00 | 6:00 | 6:00 | 6:00 | |
| 7:00 | 7:00 | 7:00 | 7:00 | 7:00 | |

| Do. Call | Do. Call | Do. Call | Do. Call | Do. Call | Do. Call |
|---|---|---|---|---|---|
| | | | | | |

| $ Money in | $ Money in | $ Money in | $ Money in | $ Money in | $ Money in |
|---|---|---|---|---|---|
| | | | | | |

## Remembering Me

I am: _____

What I love about me is: _____

_____

What I am proud of this week is: _____

_____

## Weekly Goals:

1. _____ ○    3. _____ ○

2. _____ ○    4. _____ ○

## Not to Miss:

·      ·

·      ·

## Projects to Complete:

_____

_____

_____

## Recipes to Try:

_____

_____

_____

## To Beautify my Home:

_____

_____

_____

## Call - Email - Social Media:

·      ·

·      ·

·      ·

·      ·

## To Do:

_____

_____

_____

_____

_____

### Groceries:

_____

_____

## To Buy:

·      ·

·      ·

·      ·

## My Balanced Heart

FAMILY HOLIDAY · KIND KIN DEED · COUPLES DATES · FRIENDS · HAVING FUN TOGETHER · KIND KID DEED · MY FAMILY · BESTIES · SPOUSES FAMILY · GROWING · KIDS & PETS · SPOUSE · ALONE TIME · READING · ME · SELF CARE · MASSAGE · SAVINGS · WORK · CREATIVITY · INVESTING · EXERCISE · SPIRITUAL WELL BEING · MUSIC · CARDIO · MEDITATION · WEIGHT · DEEP BREATHING · YOGA & STRETCHING · WALKING · CONTRIBUTING TO OTHERS · TIME IN NATURE

## My Weekly Reflection

## What word best describes ME this week?

# My Authentic Heart Words

| | | | | | |
|---|---|---|---|---|---|
| | | | | | |

| Workout | Ⓐ Ⓒ | Ⓐ Ⓒ | Ⓐ Ⓒ | Ⓐ Ⓒ | Ⓐ Ⓒ | Ⓐ Ⓒ |
|---|---|---|---|---|---|---|
| Just for Me | ♥ | ♥ | ♥ | ♥ | ♥ | |
| Water | ⊔⊔⊔⊔⊔⊔⊔ | ⊔⊔⊔⊔⊔⊔⊔ | ⊔⊔⊔⊔⊔⊔⊔ | ⊔⊔⊔⊔⊔⊔⊔ | ⊔⊔⊔⊔⊔⊔⊔ | ⊔⊔⊔⊔⊔⊔⊔ |
| Wins ✓ | | | | | | |
| Daily Happy Moment ☺ | | | | | | |

| MONDAY ☐ | TUESDAY ☐ | WEDNESDAY ☐ | THURSDAY ☐ | FRIDAY ☐ | SATURDAY ☐ |
|---|---|---|---|---|---|
| 7:00 | 7:00 | 7:00 | 7:00 | 7:00 | |
| 8:00 | 8:00 | 8:00 | 8:00 | 8:00 | |
| 9:00 | 9:00 | 9:00 | 9:00 | 9:00 | |
| 10:00 | 10:00 | 10:00 | 10:00 | 10:00 | |
| 11:00 | 11:00 | 11:00 | 11:00 | 11:00 | |
| 12:00 | 12:00 | 12:00 | 12:00 | 12:00 | |
| 1:00 | 1:00 | 1:00 | 1:00 | 1:00 | |
| 2:00 | 2:00 | 2:00 | 2:00 | 2:00 | SUNDAY ☐ |
| 3:00 | 3:00 | 3:00 | 3:00 | 3:00 | |
| 4:00 | 4:00 | 4:00 | 4:00 | 4:00 | |
| 5:00 | 5:00 | 5:00 | 5:00 | 5:00 | |
| 6:00 | 6:00 | 6:00 | 6:00 | 6:00 | |
| 7:00 | 7:00 | 7:00 | 7:00 | 7:00 | |

| Do. Call | Do. Call | Do. Call | Do. Call | Do. Call | Do. Call |
|---|---|---|---|---|---|
| $ Money in | $ Money in | $ Money in | $ Money in | $ Money in | $ Money in |

## Remembering Me

I am: _____

What I love about me is: _____

_____

What I am proud of this week is: _____

_____

## Weekly Goals:

1. _____ ◯   3. _____ ◯

2. _____ ◯   4. _____ ◯

## Not to Miss:

- •
- •

## Projects to Complete:

_____

_____

_____

## Recipes to Try:

_____

_____

_____

## To Beautify my Home:

_____

_____

_____

## Call - Email - Social Media:

- •          •
- •          •
- •          •
- •          •

## To Buy:

- •          •
- •          •
- •          •

## To Do:

_____  _____

_____  _____

_____

## Groceries:

_____  _____  _____

_____  _____  _____

_____  _____  _____

_____  _____  _____

*My Balanced Heart*

FAMILY HOLIDAY
KIND KIN DEED
KIND KID DEED
GROWING
READING
SAVINGS
INVESTING
CARDIO
WEIGHT
YOGA & STRETCHING
WALKING
CONTRIBUTING TO OTHERS
MY FAMILY
KIDS & PETS
WORK
EXERCISE
SPIRITUAL WELL BEING
TIME IN NATURE
DEEP BREATHING
MEDITATION
MUSIC
CREATIVITY
MASSAGE
BESTIES
SPOUSE
SELF CARE
ALONE TIME
SPOUSES FAMILY
HAVING FUN TOGETHER
FRIENDS
COUPLES DATES
ME

*My Weekly Reflection*

## What word best describes ME this week?

### This Month ♥

**Goals to Complete:**

1. _____ ○
2. _____ ○
3. _____ ○
4. _____ ○
5. _____ ○

**Places to Explore:**

_____
_____
_____
_____
_____

**To Buy:**

· _____        · _____
· _____        · _____
· _____        · _____

**Not to Miss:**

· _____        · _____
· _____        · _____
· _____        · _____

**Favorite Books I am Reading:**

· _____        · _____
· _____        · _____

# Month: _____

| SUNDAY | MONDAY | TUESDAY |
|--------|--------|---------|
|  |  |  |
|  |  |  |
|  |  |  |
|  |  |  |
|  |  |  |

### ♥ PLAN OF ACTION

| Work: | Personal: | Misc: |
|-------|-----------|-------|
| ○ _____ | ○ _____ | ○ _____ |
| ○ _____ | ○ _____ | ○ _____ |
| ○ _____ | ○ _____ | ○ _____ |
| ○ _____ | ○ _____ | ○ _____ |
| ○ _____ | ○ _____ | ○ _____ |
| ○ _____ | ○ _____ | ○ _____ |
| ○ _____ | ○ _____ | ○ _____ |
| ○ _____ | ○ _____ | ○ _____ |

*"My Happiness grows in direct proportion to my acceptance, and in inverse proportion to my expectations." ~ Michael J. Fox*

| WEDNESDAY | THURSDAY | FRIDAY | SATURDAY |
|---|---|---|---|
| | | | |
| | | | |
| | | | |
| | | | |
| | | | |

## What made my ♥ happy this month...

_____

_____

_____

_____

_____

_____

With gratitude & love, thank you.

## My Accomplishments this Month

### Improvements In My Life:
. 
. 
. 
. 

### Good Deeds Done:
. 
. 
. 
. 

### Fun and Spontaneous:
. 
. 
. 
. 

### I Treated Myself To:
. 
. 
. 
. 

### New Experiences:
. 
. 
. 
. 

### My Manifestation List:
CLAIM AS TRUE          DATE RECEIVED

1. _____    _____

2. _____    _____

3. _____    _____

4. _____    _____

5. _____    _____

# $ Keeping Track of the Flow of it All

Month: _____

| DATES + DETAILS | MONEY IN | SAVINGS | SHARING WITH OTHERS | INSURANCE + HEALTH EXPENSES | HOUSE EXPENSES | GROCERIES | TRANSPORTATION EXPENSES | ENTERTAINMENT + FUN EXPENSES | HOLIDAY EXPENSES | PERSONAL EXPENSES | DINING OUT | MISC |
|---|---|---|---|---|---|---|---|---|---|---|---|---|
| | | | | | | | | | | | | |
| | | | | | | | | | | | | |
| | | | | | | | | | | | | |
| | | | | | | | | | | | | |
| | | | | | | | | | | | | |
| | | | | | | | | | | | | |
| | | | | | | | | | | | | |
| | | | | | | | | | | | | |
| | | | | | | | | | | | | |
| | | | | | | | | | | | | |
| | | | | | | | | | | | | |
| | | | | | | | | | | | | |
| | | | | | | | | | | | | |
| | | | | | | | | | | | | |
| | | | | | | | | | | | | |
| | | | | | | | | | | | | |
| $ TOTALS | | | | | | | | | | | | |

# My Journaling Space ♥

# My Authentic Heart Words

| | | | | | |
|---|---|---|---|---|---|
| | | | | | |

| | | | | | | |
|---|---|---|---|---|---|---|
| Workout | Ⓐ Ⓒ | Ⓐ Ⓒ | Ⓐ Ⓒ | Ⓐ Ⓒ | Ⓐ Ⓒ | Ⓐ Ⓒ |
| Just for Me | ♥ | ♥ | ♥ | ♥ | ♥ | |
| Water | ⬚⬚⬚⬚⬚⬚⬚ | ⬚⬚⬚⬚⬚⬚⬚ | ⬚⬚⬚⬚⬚⬚⬚ | ⬚⬚⬚⬚⬚⬚⬚ | ⬚⬚⬚⬚⬚⬚⬚ | ⬚⬚⬚⬚⬚⬚⬚ |
| Wins ✓ | | | | | | |
| Daily Happy Moment ☺ | | | | | | |

| MONDAY ☐ | TUESDAY ☐ | WEDNESDAY ☐ | THURSDAY ☐ | FRIDAY ☐ | SATURDAY ☐ |
|---|---|---|---|---|---|
| 7:00 | 7:00 | 7:00 | 7:00 | 7:00 | |
| 8:00 | 8:00 | 8:00 | 8:00 | 8:00 | |
| 9:00 | 9:00 | 9:00 | 9:00 | 9:00 | |
| 10:00 | 10:00 | 10:00 | 10:00 | 10:00 | |
| 11:00 | 11:00 | 11:00 | 11:00 | 11:00 | |
| 12:00 | 12:00 | 12:00 | 12:00 | 12:00 | |
| 1:00 | 1:00 | 1:00 | 1:00 | 1:00 | |
| 2:00 | 2:00 | 2:00 | 2:00 | 2:00 | **SUNDAY** ☐ |
| 3:00 | 3:00 | 3:00 | 3:00 | 3:00 | |
| 4:00 | 4:00 | 4:00 | 4:00 | 4:00 | |
| 5:00 | 5:00 | 5:00 | 5:00 | 5:00 | |
| 6:00 | 6:00 | 6:00 | 6:00 | 6:00 | |
| 7:00 | 7:00 | 7:00 | 7:00 | 7:00 | |

| Do. Call | Do. Call | Do. Call | Do. Call | Do. Call | Do. Call |
|---|---|---|---|---|---|
| | | | | | |

| $ Money in | $ Money in | $ Money in | $ Money in | $ Money in | $ Money in |
|---|---|---|---|---|---|
| | | | | | |

## Remembering Me

I am: _____

What I love about me is: _____

_____

What I am proud of this week is: _____

_____

## Weekly Goals:

1. _____ ○   3. _____ ○

2. _____ ○   4. _____ ○

## Not to Miss:

·                    ·

·                    ·

## Projects to Complete:

_____

_____

_____

_____

## Recipes to Try:

_____

_____

_____

_____

## To Beautify my Home:

_____

_____

_____

_____

## Call - Email - Social Media:

·                    ·

·                    ·

·                    ·

·                    ·

## To Do:

_____  _____

_____  _____

_____  ## Groceries:

_____  _____

_____  _____

## To Buy:

·                    ·

·                    ·

·                    ·

*My Balanced Heart*

*My Weekly Reflection*

## What word best describes ME this week?

# My Authentic Heart Words

|  | | | | | |
|---|---|---|---|---|---|
| | | | | | |

| | Ⓐ Ⓒ | Ⓐ Ⓒ | Ⓐ Ⓒ | Ⓐ Ⓒ | Ⓐ Ⓒ | Ⓐ Ⓒ |
|---|---|---|---|---|---|---|
| Workout | | | | | | |
| Just for Me | ♥ | ♥ | ♥ | ♥ | ♥ | |
| Water | ⊔⊔⊔⊔⊔⊔ | ⊔⊔⊔⊔⊔⊔ | ⊔⊔⊔⊔⊔⊔ | ⊔⊔⊔⊔⊔⊔ | ⊔⊔⊔⊔⊔⊔ | ⊔⊔⊔⊔⊔⊔ |
| Wins ✓ | | | | | | |
| Daily Happy Moment ☺ | | | | | | |

| MONDAY ☐ | TUESDAY ☐ | WEDNESDAY ☐ | THURSDAY ☐ | FRIDAY ☐ | SATURDAY ☐ |
|---|---|---|---|---|---|
| 7:00 | 7:00 | 7:00 | 7:00 | 7:00 | |
| 8:00 | 8:00 | 8:00 | 8:00 | 8:00 | |
| 9:00 | 9:00 | 9:00 | 9:00 | 9:00 | |
| 10:00 | 10:00 | 10:00 | 10:00 | 10:00 | |
| 11:00 | 11:00 | 11:00 | 11:00 | 11:00 | |
| 12:00 | 12:00 | 12:00 | 12:00 | 12:00 | |
| 1:00 | 1:00 | 1:00 | 1:00 | 1:00 | |
| 2:00 | 2:00 | 2:00 | 2:00 | 2:00 | SUNDAY ☐ |
| 3:00 | 3:00 | 3:00 | 3:00 | 3:00 | |
| 4:00 | 4:00 | 4:00 | 4:00 | 4:00 | |
| 5:00 | 5:00 | 5:00 | 5:00 | 5:00 | |
| 6:00 | 6:00 | 6:00 | 6:00 | 6:00 | |
| 7:00 | 7:00 | 7:00 | 7:00 | 7:00 | |

| Do. Call | Do. Call | Do. Call | Do. Call | Do. Call | Do. Call |
|---|---|---|---|---|---|
| | | | | | |

| $ Money in | $ Money in | $ Money in | $ Money in | $ Money in | $ Money in |
|---|---|---|---|---|---|
| | | | | | |

## Remembering Me

I am: _____

What I love about me is: _____

_____

What I am proud of this week is: _____

_____

## Weekly Goals:

1. _____ ○   3. _____ ○

2. _____ ○   4. _____ ○

## Not to Miss:

· _____   · _____

· _____   · _____

## Projects to Complete:

_____

_____

_____

## Recipes to Try:

_____

_____

_____

## To Beautify my Home:

_____

_____

_____

## Call - Email - Social Media:

· _____   · _____

· _____   · _____

· _____   · _____

· _____   · _____

## To Buy:

· _____   · _____

· _____   · _____

## To Do:

_____   _____

_____   _____

_____   

### Groceries:

_____   _____

_____   _____

_____   _____

_____   _____

_____   _____

### My Balanced Heart

FAMILY HOLIDAY • KIND KIN DEED • COUPLES DATES • FRIENDS • HAVING FUN TOGETHER • KIND KID DEED • MY FAMILY • BESTIES • SPOUSES FAMILY • GROWING • KIDS & PETS • SPOUSE • ALONE TIME • READING • ME • SELF CARE • MASSAGE • SAVINGS • WORK • CREATIVITY • INVESTING • EXERCISE • SPIRITUAL WELL BEING • MUSIC • CARDIO • MEDITATION • WEIGHT • DEEP BREATHING • YOGA & STRETCHING • WALKING • CONTRIBUTING TO OTHERS • TIME IN NATURE

### My Weekly Reflection

### What word best describes ME this week?

119

# My Authentic Heart Words

| | | | | | |
|---|---|---|---|---|---|
| | | | | | |

| | | Ⓐ Ⓒ | Ⓐ Ⓒ | Ⓐ Ⓒ | Ⓐ Ⓒ | Ⓐ Ⓒ | Ⓐ Ⓒ |
|---|---|---|---|---|---|

**Workout** Ⓐ Ⓒ    Ⓐ Ⓒ    Ⓐ Ⓒ    Ⓐ Ⓒ    Ⓐ Ⓒ    Ⓐ Ⓒ

**Just for Me** ♥    ♥    ♥    ♥    ♥

**Water**  ⬚⬚⬚⬚⬚⬚  ⬚⬚⬚⬚⬚⬚  ⬚⬚⬚⬚⬚⬚  ⬚⬚⬚⬚⬚⬚  ⬚⬚⬚⬚⬚⬚  ⬚⬚⬚⬚⬚⬚

**Wins ✓**

**Daily Happy Moment ☺**

| MONDAY ☐ | TUESDAY ☐ | WEDNESDAY ☐ | THURSDAY ☐ | FRIDAY ☐ | SATURDAY ☐ |
|---|---|---|---|---|---|
| 7:00 | 7:00 | 7:00 | 7:00 | 7:00 | |
| 8:00 | 8:00 | 8:00 | 8:00 | 8:00 | |
| 9:00 | 9:00 | 9:00 | 9:00 | 9:00 | |
| 10:00 | 10:00 | 10:00 | 10:00 | 10:00 | |
| 11:00 | 11:00 | 11:00 | 11:00 | 11:00 | |
| 12:00 | 12:00 | 12:00 | 12:00 | 12:00 | |
| 1:00 | 1:00 | 1:00 | 1:00 | 1:00 | |
| 2:00 | 2:00 | 2:00 | 2:00 | 2:00 | SUNDAY ☐ |
| 3:00 | 3:00 | 3:00 | 3:00 | 3:00 | |
| 4:00 | 4:00 | 4:00 | 4:00 | 4:00 | |
| 5:00 | 5:00 | 5:00 | 5:00 | 5:00 | |
| 6:00 | 6:00 | 6:00 | 6:00 | 6:00 | |
| 7:00 | 7:00 | 7:00 | 7:00 | 7:00 | |

| Do. Call | Do. Call | Do. Call | Do. Call | Do. Call | Do. Call |
|---|---|---|---|---|---|
| | | | | | |

| $ Money in | $ Money in | $ Money in | $ Money in | $ Money in | $ Money in |
|---|---|---|---|---|---|
| | | | | | |

## Remembering Me

I am: _____

What I love about me is: _____

_____

What I am proud of this week is: _____

_____

## Weekly Goals:

1. _____ ○   3. _____ ○

2. _____ ○   4. _____ ○

## Not to Miss:

· _____   · _____

· _____   · _____

## Projects to Complete:

_____

_____

_____

_____

## Recipes to Try:

_____

_____

_____

## To Beautify my Home:

_____

_____

_____

_____

## Call - Email - Social Media:

· _____   · _____

· _____   · _____

· _____   · _____

· _____   · _____

## To Buy:

· _____   · _____

· _____   · _____

· _____   · _____

## To Do:

_____

_____

_____

_____

## Groceries:

_____ _____

_____ _____

_____ _____

## My Balanced Heart

KIND KIN DEED
FAMILY HOLIDAY
COUPLES DATES
FRIENDS
HAVING FUN TOGETHER
MY FAMILY
BESTIES
SPOUSES FAMILY
KIND KID DEED
KIDS & PETS
SPOUSE
ALONE TIME
ME
GROWING
SELF CARE
MASSAGE
READING
WORK
CREATIVITY
SAVINGS
EXERCISE
SPIRITUAL WELL BEING
MUSIC
INVESTING
CARDIO
MEDITATION
WEIGHT
DEEP BREATHING
YOGA & STRETCHING
WALKING
TIME IN NATURE
CONTRIBUTING TO OTHERS

## My Weekly Reflection

## What word best describes ME this week?

# My Authentic Heart Words

|  |  |  |  |  |  |
|---|---|---|---|---|---|
|  |  |  |  |  |  |

| | | | | | | |
|---|---|---|---|---|---|---|
| Workout | Ⓐ Ⓒ | Ⓐ Ⓒ | Ⓐ Ⓒ | Ⓐ Ⓒ | Ⓐ Ⓒ | Ⓐ Ⓒ |
| Just for Me | ♥ | ♥ | ♥ | ♥ | ♥ | |
| Water | □□□□□□□ | □□□□□□□ | □□□□□□□ | □□□□□□□ | □□□□□□□ | □□□□□□□ |
| Wins ✓ | | | | | | |
| Daily Happy Moment ☺ | | | | | | |

| MONDAY ☐ | TUESDAY ☐ | WEDNESDAY ☐ | THURSDAY ☐ | FRIDAY ☐ | SATURDAY ☐ |
|---|---|---|---|---|---|
| 7:00 | 7:00 | 7:00 | 7:00 | 7:00 | |
| 8:00 | 8:00 | 8:00 | 8:00 | 8:00 | |
| 9:00 | 9:00 | 9:00 | 9:00 | 9:00 | |
| 10:00 | 10:00 | 10:00 | 10:00 | 10:00 | |
| 11:00 | 11:00 | 11:00 | 11:00 | 11:00 | |
| 12:00 | 12:00 | 12:00 | 12:00 | 12:00 | |
| 1:00 | 1:00 | 1:00 | 1:00 | 1:00 | |
| 2:00 | 2:00 | 2:00 | 2:00 | 2:00 | SUNDAY ☐ |
| 3:00 | 3:00 | 3:00 | 3:00 | 3:00 | |
| 4:00 | 4:00 | 4:00 | 4:00 | 4:00 | |
| 5:00 | 5:00 | 5:00 | 5:00 | 5:00 | |
| 6:00 | 6:00 | 6:00 | 6:00 | 6:00 | |
| 7:00 | 7:00 | 7:00 | 7:00 | 7:00 | |

| Do. Call | Do. Call | Do. Call | Do. Call | Do. Call | Do. Call |
|---|---|---|---|---|---|
| | | | | | |

| $ Money in | $ Money in | $ Money in | $ Money in | $ Money in | $ Money in |
|---|---|---|---|---|---|
| | | | | | |

## Remembering Me

I am: _____

What I love about me is: _____

_____

What I am proud of this week is: _____

_____

## Weekly Goals:

1. _____ ○  3. _____ ○

2. _____ ○  4. _____ ○

## Not to Miss:

·      ·

·      ·

## Projects to Complete:

_____

_____

_____

_____

## Recipes to Try:

_____

_____

_____

_____

## To Beautify my Home:

_____

_____

_____

_____

## Call - Email - Social Media:

·      ·

·      ·

·      ·

·      ·

## To Do:

_____

_____

_____

## Groceries:

_____

_____

_____

## To Buy:

·      ·

·      ·

·      ·

### My Balanced Heart

KIND KIN DEED · FAMILY HOLIDAY · KIND KID DEED · GROWING · READING · SAVINGS · INVESTING · CARDIO · WEIGHT · YOGA & STRETCHING · WALKING · CONTRIBUTING TO OTHERS · TIME IN NATURE · DEEP BREATHING · MEDITATION · MUSIC · CREATIVITY · MASSAGE · ALONE TIME · SPOUSES FAMILY · HAVING FUN TOGETHER · FRIENDS · COUPLES DATES

MY FAMILY · BESTIES · KIDS & PETS · SPOUSE · WORK · EXERCISE · SPIRITUAL WELL BEING · SELF CARE

ME

### My Weekly Reflection

## What word best describes ME this week?

123

# My Authentic Heart Words

| | | | | | |
|---|---|---|---|---|---|
| | | | | | |

| Workout | Ⓐ Ⓒ | Ⓐ Ⓒ | Ⓐ Ⓒ | Ⓐ Ⓒ | Ⓐ Ⓒ | Ⓐ Ⓒ |
|---|---|---|---|---|---|---|
| Just for Me | ♥ | ♥ | ♥ | ♥ | ♥ | |
| Water | ▯▯▯▯▯▯▯ | ▯▯▯▯▯▯▯ | ▯▯▯▯▯▯▯ | ▯▯▯▯▯▯▯ | ▯▯▯▯▯▯▯ | ▯▯▯▯▯▯▯ |
| Wins ✓ | | | | | | |
| Daily Happy Moment ☺ | | | | | | |

| MONDAY ☐ | TUESDAY ☐ | WEDNESDAY ☐ | THURSDAY ☐ | FRIDAY ☐ | SATURDAY ☐ |
|---|---|---|---|---|---|
| 7:00 | 7:00 | 7:00 | 7:00 | 7:00 | |
| 8:00 | 8:00 | 8:00 | 8:00 | 8:00 | |
| 9:00 | 9:00 | 9:00 | 9:00 | 9:00 | |
| 10:00 | 10:00 | 10:00 | 10:00 | 10:00 | |
| 11:00 | 11:00 | 11:00 | 11:00 | 11:00 | |
| 12:00 | 12:00 | 12:00 | 12:00 | 12:00 | |
| 1:00 | 1:00 | 1:00 | 1:00 | 1:00 | |
| 2:00 | 2:00 | 2:00 | 2:00 | 2:00 | SUNDAY ☐ |
| 3:00 | 3:00 | 3:00 | 3:00 | 3:00 | |
| 4:00 | 4:00 | 4:00 | 4:00 | 4:00 | |
| 5:00 | 5:00 | 5:00 | 5:00 | 5:00 | |
| 6:00 | 6:00 | 6:00 | 6:00 | 6:00 | |
| 7:00 | 7:00 | 7:00 | 7:00 | 7:00 | |

| Do. Call | Do. Call | Do. Call | Do. Call | Do. Call | Do. Call |
|---|---|---|---|---|---|
| $ Money in | $ Money in | $ Money in | $ Money in | $ Money in | $ Money in |

## Remembering Me

I am: _____

What I love about me is: _____

_____

What I am proud of this week is: _____

_____

## Weekly Goals:

1. _____ ○   3. _____ ○

2. _____ ○   4. _____ ○

## Not to Miss:

· 

·

· 

·

## Projects to Complete:

_____

_____

_____

_____

## Recipes to Try:

_____

_____

_____

_____

## To Beautify my Home:

_____

_____

_____

_____

## Call - Email - Social Media:

·              ·

·              ·

·              ·

·              ·

## To Buy:

·              ·

·              ·

·              ·

## To Do:

_____

_____

_____

_____

_____

_____

### Groceries:

_____

_____

_____

_____

_____

*My Balanced Heart*

*My Weekly Reflection*

What word best describes ME this week?

**This Month ♥**

## Goals to Complete:

1. _____ ○
2. _____ ○
3. _____ ○
4. _____ ○
5. _____ ○

## Places to Explore:

_____
_____
_____
_____
_____

## To Buy:

·  _____      ·  _____
·  _____      ·  _____
·  _____      ·  _____

## Not to Miss:

·  _____      ·  _____
·  _____      ·  _____
·  _____      ·  _____

## Favorite Books I am Reading:

·  _____      ·  _____
·  _____      ·  _____

# Month: _____

| SUNDAY | MONDAY | TUESDAY |
|---|---|---|
|  |  |  |
|  |  |  |
|  |  |  |
|  |  |  |
|  |  |  |

## ♥ PLAN OF ACTION

| Work: | Personal: | Misc: |
|---|---|---|
| ○ _____ | ○ _____ | ○ _____ |
| ○ _____ | ○ _____ | ○ _____ |
| ○ _____ | ○ _____ | ○ _____ |
| ○ _____ | ○ _____ | ○ _____ |
| ○ _____ | ○ _____ | ○ _____ |
| ○ _____ | ○ _____ | ○ _____ |
| ○ _____ | ○ _____ | ○ _____ |
| ○ _____ | ○ _____ | ○ _____ |

*"If you want to be happy, be."* ~ Leo Tolstoy

| WEDNESDAY | THURSDAY | FRIDAY | SATURDAY |
|---|---|---|---|
|  |  |  |  |
|  |  |  |  |
|  |  |  |  |
|  |  |  |  |
|  |  |  |  |

## What made my ♥ happy this month...

_____

_____

_____

_____

_____

_____

_____

With gratitude & love, thank you.

## My Accomplishments this Month

### Improvements In My Life:
· 
· 
· 
· 

### Good Deeds Done:
· 
· 
· 
· 

### Fun and Spontaneous:
· 
· 
· 
· 

### I Treated Myself To:
· 
· 
· 
· 

### New Experiences:
· 
· 
· 
· 

### My Manifestation List:

| | CLAIM AS TRUE | DATE RECEIVED |
|---|---|---|
| 1. | _____ | _____ |
| 2. | _____ | _____ |
| 3. | _____ | _____ |
| 4. | _____ | _____ |
| 5. | _____ | _____ |

# $ Keeping Track of the Flow of it All

Month: _____

| DATES + DETAILS | MONEY IN | SAVINGS | SHARING WITH OTHERS | INSURANCE + HEALTH EXPENSES | HOUSE EXPENSES | GROCERIES | TRANSPORTATION EXPENSES | ENTERTAINMENT + FUN EXPENSES | HOLIDAY EXPENSES | PERSONAL EXPENSES | DINING OUT | MISC |
|---|---|---|---|---|---|---|---|---|---|---|---|---|
| | | | | | | | | | | | | |
| | | | | | | | | | | | | |
| | | | | | | | | | | | | |
| | | | | | | | | | | | | |
| | | | | | | | | | | | | |
| | | | | | | | | | | | | |
| | | | | | | | | | | | | |
| | | | | | | | | | | | | |
| | | | | | | | | | | | | |
| | | | | | | | | | | | | |
| | | | | | | | | | | | | |
| | | | | | | | | | | | | |
| | | | | | | | | | | | | |
| | | | | | | | | | | | | |
| | | | | | | | | | | | | |
| $ TOTALS | | | | | | | | | | | | |

# My Journaling Space ♥

# My Authentic Heart Words

| | | | | | |
|---|---|---|---|---|---|
| | | | | | |

| | | | | | | |
|---|---|---|---|---|---|---|
| Workout | Ⓐ Ⓒ | Ⓐ Ⓒ | Ⓐ Ⓒ | Ⓐ Ⓒ | Ⓐ Ⓒ | Ⓐ Ⓒ |
| Just for Me | ♥ | ♥ | ♥ | ♥ | ♥ | |
| Water | ⬜⬜⬜⬜⬜⬜⬜ | ⬜⬜⬜⬜⬜⬜⬜ | ⬜⬜⬜⬜⬜⬜⬜ | ⬜⬜⬜⬜⬜⬜⬜ | ⬜⬜⬜⬜⬜⬜⬜ | ⬜⬜⬜⬜⬜⬜⬜ |
| Wins ✓ | | | | | | |
| Daily Happy Moment ☺ | | | | | | |

| MONDAY ☐ | TUESDAY ☐ | WEDNESDAY ☐ | THURSDAY ☐ | FRIDAY ☐ | SATURDAY ☐ |
|---|---|---|---|---|---|
| 7:00 | 7:00 | 7:00 | 7:00 | 7:00 | |
| 8:00 | 8:00 | 8:00 | 8:00 | 8:00 | |
| 9:00 | 9:00 | 9:00 | 9:00 | 9:00 | |
| 10:00 | 10:00 | 10:00 | 10:00 | 10:00 | |
| 11:00 | 11:00 | 11:00 | 11:00 | 11:00 | |
| 12:00 | 12:00 | 12:00 | 12:00 | 12:00 | |
| 1:00 | 1:00 | 1:00 | 1:00 | 1:00 | |
| 2:00 | 2:00 | 2:00 | 2:00 | 2:00 | SUNDAY ☐ |
| 3:00 | 3:00 | 3:00 | 3:00 | 3:00 | |
| 4:00 | 4:00 | 4:00 | 4:00 | 4:00 | |
| 5:00 | 5:00 | 5:00 | 5:00 | 5:00 | |
| 6:00 | 6:00 | 6:00 | 6:00 | 6:00 | |
| 7:00 | 7:00 | 7:00 | 7:00 | 7:00 | |

| Do. Call | Do. Call | Do. Call | Do. Call | Do. Call | Do. Call |
|---|---|---|---|---|---|
| | | | | | |

| $ Money in | $ Money in | $ Money in | $ Money in | $ Money in | $ Money in |
|---|---|---|---|---|---|
| | | | | | |

## Remembering Me

I am: _____

What I love about me is: _____

_____

What I am proud of this week is: _____

_____

## Weekly Goals:

1. _____ ○   3. _____ ○

2. _____ ○   4. _____ ○

## Not to Miss:

· _____     · _____

· _____     · _____

## Projects to Complete:

_____

_____

_____

_____

## Recipes to Try:

_____

_____

_____

_____

## To Beautify my Home:

_____

_____

_____

_____

## Call - Email - Social Media:

· _____     · _____

· _____     · _____

· _____     · _____

· _____     · _____

## To Do:

_____

_____

_____

### Groceries:

_____

_____

_____

## To Buy:

· _____     · _____

· _____     · _____

*My Balanced Heart*

FAMILY HOLIDAY
KIND KIN DEED
COUPLES DATES
FRIENDS
HAVING FUN TOGETHER
KIND KID DEED
MY FAMILY
BESTIES
SPOUSES FAMILY
GROWING
KIDS & PETS
SPOUSE
ALONE TIME
READING
ME
SELF CARE
MASSAGE
WORK
SAVINGS
CREATIVITY
INVESTING
EXERCISE
SPIRITUAL WELL BEING
MUSIC
CARDIO
MEDITATION
WEIGHT
DEEP BREATHING
YOGA & STRETCHING
WALKING
TIME IN NATURE
CONTRIBUTING TO OTHERS

*My Weekly Reflection*

## What word best describes ME this week?

# My Authentic Heart Words

| | | | | | |
|---|---|---|---|---|---|
| | | | | | |

| | | | | | | |
|---|---|---|---|---|---|---|
| Workout | Ⓐ Ⓒ | Ⓐ Ⓒ | Ⓐ Ⓒ | Ⓐ Ⓒ | Ⓐ Ⓒ | Ⓐ Ⓒ |
| Just for Me | ♥ | ♥ | ♥ | ♥ | ♥ | |
| Water | ▢▢▢▢▢▢▢ | ▢▢▢▢▢▢▢ | ▢▢▢▢▢▢▢ | ▢▢▢▢▢▢▢ | ▢▢▢▢▢▢▢ | ▢▢▢▢▢▢▢ |
| Wins ✓ | | | | | | |
| Daily Happy Moment ☺ | | | | | | |

| MONDAY ☐ | TUESDAY ☐ | WEDNESDAY ☐ | THURSDAY ☐ | FRIDAY ☐ | SATURDAY ☐ |
|---|---|---|---|---|---|
| 7:00 | 7:00 | 7:00 | 7:00 | 7:00 | |
| 8:00 | 8:00 | 8:00 | 8:00 | 8:00 | |
| 9:00 | 9:00 | 9:00 | 9:00 | 9:00 | |
| 10:00 | 10:00 | 10:00 | 10:00 | 10:00 | |
| 11:00 | 11:00 | 11:00 | 11:00 | 11:00 | |
| 12:00 | 12:00 | 12:00 | 12:00 | 12:00 | |
| 1:00 | 1:00 | 1:00 | 1:00 | 1:00 | |
| 2:00 | 2:00 | 2:00 | 2:00 | 2:00 | SUNDAY ☐ |
| 3:00 | 3:00 | 3:00 | 3:00 | 3:00 | |
| 4:00 | 4:00 | 4:00 | 4:00 | 4:00 | |
| 5:00 | 5:00 | 5:00 | 5:00 | 5:00 | |
| 6:00 | 6:00 | 6:00 | 6:00 | 6:00 | |
| 7:00 | 7:00 | 7:00 | 7:00 | 7:00 | |

| Do. Call | Do. Call | Do. Call | Do. Call | Do. Call | Do. Call |
|---|---|---|---|---|---|
| | | | | | |

| $ Money in | $ Money in | $ Money in | $ Money in | $ Money in | $ Money in |
|---|---|---|---|---|---|
| | | | | | |

## Remembering Me

I am: _____

What I love about me is: _____

_____

What I am proud of this week is: _____

_____

## Weekly Goals:

1. _____ ○    3. _____ ○

2. _____ ○    4. _____ ○

## Not to Miss:

· _____     · _____

· _____     · _____

## Projects to Complete:

_____

_____

_____

_____

## Recipes to Try:

_____

_____

_____

_____

## To Beautify my Home:

_____

_____

_____

_____

## Call - Email - Social Media:

· _____     · _____

· _____     · _____

· _____     · _____

· _____     · _____

## To Do:

_____     _____

_____     _____

_____     

_____     ### Groceries:

_____     _____ _____

_____     _____ _____

_____     _____ _____

_____     _____ _____

## To Buy:

· _____     · _____

· _____     · _____

· _____     · _____

*My Balanced Heart*

FAMILY HOLIDAY · KIND KIN DEED · COUPLES DATES · FRIENDS · HAVING FUN TOGETHER · KIND KID DEED · MY FAMILY · BESTIES · SPOUSES FAMILY · KIDS & PETS · SPOUSE · ALONE TIME · GROWING · ME · SELF CARE · MASSAGE · READING · WORK · CREATIVITY · SAVINGS · EXERCISE · SPIRITUAL WELL BEING · MUSIC · INVESTING · CARDIO · MEDITATION · WEIGHT · DEEP BREATHING · YOGA & STRETCHING · WALKING · TIME IN NATURE · CONTRIBUTING TO OTHERS

*My Weekly Reflection*

## What word best describes ME this week?

# My Authentic Heart Words

| | | | | | |
|---|---|---|---|---|---|
| | | | | | |

| | | | | | | |
|---|---|---|---|---|---|---|
| Workout Ⓐ Ⓒ | | Ⓐ Ⓒ | Ⓐ Ⓒ | Ⓐ Ⓒ | Ⓐ Ⓒ | Ⓐ Ⓒ |
| Just for Me | ♥ | ♥ | ♥ | ♥ | ♥ | |
| Water | ⊔⊔⊔⊔⊔⊔⊔ | ⊔⊔⊔⊔⊔⊔⊔ | ⊔⊔⊔⊔⊔⊔⊔ | ⊔⊔⊔⊔⊔⊔⊔ | ⊔⊔⊔⊔⊔⊔⊔ | ⊔⊔⊔⊔⊔⊔⊔ |
| Wins ✓ | | | | | | |
| Daily Happy Moment ☺ | | | | | | |

| MONDAY ☐ | TUESDAY ☐ | WEDNESDAY ☐ | THURSDAY ☐ | FRIDAY ☐ | SATURDAY ☐ |
|---|---|---|---|---|---|
| 7:00 | 7:00 | 7:00 | 7:00 | 7:00 | |
| 8:00 | 8:00 | 8:00 | 8:00 | 8:00 | |
| 9:00 | 9:00 | 9:00 | 9:00 | 9:00 | |
| 10:00 | 10:00 | 10:00 | 10:00 | 10:00 | |
| 11:00 | 11:00 | 11:00 | 11:00 | 11:00 | |
| 12:00 | 12:00 | 12:00 | 12:00 | 12:00 | |
| 1:00 | 1:00 | 1:00 | 1:00 | 1:00 | |
| 2:00 | 2:00 | 2:00 | 2:00 | 2:00 | SUNDAY ☐ |
| 3:00 | 3:00 | 3:00 | 3:00 | 3:00 | |
| 4:00 | 4:00 | 4:00 | 4:00 | 4:00 | |
| 5:00 | 5:00 | 5:00 | 5:00 | 5:00 | |
| 6:00 | 6:00 | 6:00 | 6:00 | 6:00 | |
| 7:00 | 7:00 | 7:00 | 7:00 | 7:00 | |

| Do. Call | Do. Call | Do. Call | Do. Call | Do. Call | Do. Call |
|---|---|---|---|---|---|
| | | | | | |

| $ Money in | $ Money in | $ Money in | $ Money in | $ Money in | $ Money in |
|---|---|---|---|---|---|
| | | | | | |

## Remembering Me

I am: _____

What I love about me is: _____

_____

What I am proud of this week is: _____

_____

## Weekly Goals:

1. _____ ○   3. _____ ○

2. _____ ○   4. _____ ○

## Not to Miss:

- · _____   · _____
- · _____   · _____

## Projects to Complete:

_____

_____

_____

_____

## Recipes to Try:

_____

_____

_____

_____

## To Beautify my Home:

_____

_____

_____

_____

## Call - Email - Social Media:

- · _____   · _____
- · _____   · _____
- · _____   · _____
- · _____   · _____

## To Do:

_____   _____

_____   _____

_____   _____

### Groceries:

_____   _____

_____   _____

_____   _____

_____   _____

## To Buy:

- · _____   · _____
- · _____   · _____
- · _____   · _____

### My Balanced Heart

COUPLES DATES, FRIENDS, HAVING FUN TOGETHER, SPOUSES FAMILY, ALONE TIME, MASSAGE, CREATIVITY, MUSIC, MEDITATION, DEEP BREATHING, TIME IN NATURE, CONTRIBUTING TO OTHERS, WALKING, YOGA & STRETCHING, WEIGHT, CARDIO, INVESTING, SAVINGS, READING, GROWING, KIND KID DEED, FAMILY HOLIDAY, KIND KIN DEED

MY FAMILY, BESTIES, KIDS & PETS, SPOUSE, ME, SELF CARE, WORK, EXERCISE, SPIRITUAL WELL BEING

### My Weekly Reflection

### What word best describes ME this week?

# My Authentic Heart Words

| | | | | | |
|---|---|---|---|---|---|
| | | | | | |

| | | | | | | |
|---|---|---|---|---|---|---|
| Workout | Ⓐ Ⓒ | Ⓐ Ⓒ | Ⓐ Ⓒ | Ⓐ Ⓒ | Ⓐ Ⓒ | Ⓐ Ⓒ |
| Just for Me | ♥ | ♥ | ♥ | ♥ | ♥ | |
| Water | ▭▭▭▭▭▭▭ | ▭▭▭▭▭▭▭ | ▭▭▭▭▭▭▭ | ▭▭▭▭▭▭▭ | ▭▭▭▭▭▭▭ | ▭▭▭▭▭▭▭ |
| Wins ✓ | | | | | | |
| Daily Happy Moment ☺ | | | | | | |

| **MONDAY** ☐ | **TUESDAY** ☐ | **WEDNESDAY** ☐ | **THURSDAY** ☐ | **FRIDAY** ☐ | **SATURDAY** ☐ |
|---|---|---|---|---|---|
| 7:00 | 7:00 | 7:00 | 7:00 | 7:00 | |
| 8:00 | 8:00 | 8:00 | 8:00 | 8:00 | |
| 9:00 | 9:00 | 9:00 | 9:00 | 9:00 | |
| 10:00 | 10:00 | 10:00 | 10:00 | 10:00 | |
| 11:00 | 11:00 | 11:00 | 11:00 | 11:00 | |
| 12:00 | 12:00 | 12:00 | 12:00 | 12:00 | |
| 1:00 | 1:00 | 1:00 | 1:00 | 1:00 | |
| 2:00 | 2:00 | 2:00 | 2:00 | 2:00 | **SUNDAY** ☐ |
| 3:00 | 3:00 | 3:00 | 3:00 | 3:00 | |
| 4:00 | 4:00 | 4:00 | 4:00 | 4:00 | |
| 5:00 | 5:00 | 5:00 | 5:00 | 5:00 | |
| 6:00 | 6:00 | 6:00 | 6:00 | 6:00 | |
| 7:00 | 7:00 | 7:00 | 7:00 | 7:00 | |

| Do. Call | Do. Call | Do. Call | Do. Call | Do. Call | Do. Call |
|---|---|---|---|---|---|
| | | | | | |

| $ Money in | $ Money in | $ Money in | $ Money in | $ Money in | $ Money in |
|---|---|---|---|---|---|
| | | | | | |

## Remembering Me

I am: _____

What I love about me is: _____

_____

What I am proud of this week is: _____

_____

## Weekly Goals:

1. _____ ○   3. _____ ○

2. _____ ○   4. _____ ○

## Not to Miss:

· _____    · _____

· _____    · _____

## Projects to Complete:

_____

_____

_____

_____

## Recipes to Try:

_____

_____

_____

## To Beautify my Home:

_____

_____

_____

_____

## Call - Email - Social Media:

· _____    · _____

· _____    · _____

· _____    · _____

· _____    · _____

## To Do:

_____

_____

_____

_____

_____

_____

_____

## Groceries:

_____

_____

_____

_____

## To Buy:

· _____    · _____

· _____    · _____

· _____    · _____

My Balanced Heart

MY FAMILY · BESTIES · KIND KIN DEED · FAMILY HOLIDAY · COUPLES DATES · FRIENDS · HAVING FUN TOGETHER · SPOUSES FAMILY · SPOUSE · ALONE TIME · KIDS & PETS · KIND KID DEED · GROWING · READING · SAVINGS · INVESTING · WORK · ME · SELF CARE · MASSAGE · CREATIVITY · MUSIC · MEDITATION · SPIRITUAL WELL BEING · EXERCISE · CARDIO · WEIGHT · YOGA & STRETCHING · WALKING · CONTRIBUTING TO OTHERS · TIME IN NATURE · DEEP BREATHING

My Weekly Reflection

## What word best describes ME this week?

# My Authentic Heart Words

| | | | | | |
|---|---|---|---|---|---|

| | | | | | | |
|---|---|---|---|---|---|---|
| Workout | Ⓐ Ⓒ | Ⓐ Ⓒ | Ⓐ Ⓒ | Ⓐ Ⓒ | Ⓐ Ⓒ | Ⓐ Ⓒ |
| Just for Me | ♥ | ♥ | ♥ | ♥ | ♥ | |
| Water | | | | | | |
| Wins ✓ | | | | | | |
| Daily Happy Moment ☺ | | | | | | |

| MONDAY ☐ | TUESDAY ☐ | WEDNESDAY ☐ | THURSDAY ☐ | FRIDAY ☐ | SATURDAY ☐ |
|---|---|---|---|---|---|
| 7:00 | 7:00 | 7:00 | 7:00 | 7:00 | |
| 8:00 | 8:00 | 8:00 | 8:00 | 8:00 | |
| 9:00 | 9:00 | 9:00 | 9:00 | 9:00 | |
| 10:00 | 10:00 | 10:00 | 10:00 | 10:00 | |
| 11:00 | 11:00 | 11:00 | 11:00 | 11:00 | |
| 12:00 | 12:00 | 12:00 | 12:00 | 12:00 | |
| 1:00 | 1:00 | 1:00 | 1:00 | 1:00 | |
| 2:00 | 2:00 | 2:00 | 2:00 | 2:00 | SUNDAY ☐ |
| 3:00 | 3:00 | 3:00 | 3:00 | 3:00 | |
| 4:00 | 4:00 | 4:00 | 4:00 | 4:00 | |
| 5:00 | 5:00 | 5:00 | 5:00 | 5:00 | |
| 6:00 | 6:00 | 6:00 | 6:00 | 6:00 | |
| 7:00 | 7:00 | 7:00 | 7:00 | 7:00 | |

| Do. Call | Do. Call | Do. Call | Do. Call | Do. Call | Do. Call |
|---|---|---|---|---|---|
| | | | | | |

| $ Money in | $ Money in | $ Money in | $ Money in | $ Money in | $ Money in |
|---|---|---|---|---|---|
| | | | | | |

## Remembering Me

I am: _____

What I love about me is: _____

_____

What I am proud of this week is: _____

_____

## Weekly Goals:

1. _____ ○   3. _____ ○

2. _____ ○   4. _____ ○

## Not to Miss:

- _____      · _____
- _____      · _____

## Projects to Complete:

_____

_____

_____

_____

## Recipes to Try:

_____

_____

_____

_____

## To Beautify my Home:

_____

_____

_____

_____

## Call - Email - Social Media:

- ·
- ·
- ·
- ·

## To Buy:

- ·
- ·
- ·

## To Do:

_____      _____

_____      _____

_____      _____

### Groceries:

_____      _____

_____      _____

_____      _____

_____      _____

## My Balanced Heart

KIND KIN DEED · FAMILY HOLIDAY · COUPLES DATES · FRIENDS · HAVING FUN TOGETHER · MY FAMILY · BESTIES · SPOUSES FAMILY · KIND KID DEED · KIDS & PETS · SPOUSE · ALONE TIME · GROWING · ME · SELF CARE · MASSAGE · READING · WORK · CREATIVITY · SAVINGS · EXERCISE · SPIRITUAL WELL BEING · MUSIC · INVESTING · CARDIO · MEDITATION · WEIGHT · DEEP BREATHING · YOGA & STRETCHING · WALKING · TIME IN NATURE · CONTRIBUTING TO OTHERS

## My Weekly Reflection

## What word best describes ME this week?

## This Month ♥

### Goals to Complete:
1. _____ ◯
2. _____ ◯
3. _____ ◯
4. _____ ◯
5. _____ ◯

### Places to Explore:
_____
_____
_____
_____
_____

### To Buy:
·      ·
·      ·
·      ·

### Not to Miss:
·      ·
·      ·
·      ·

### Favorite Books I am Reading:
·      ·
·      ·

# Month: _____

| SUNDAY | MONDAY | TUESDAY |
|--------|--------|---------|
|        |        |         |
|        |        |         |
|        |        |         |
|        |        |         |
|        |        |         |

## ♥ PLAN OF ACTION

| Work: | Personal: | Misc: |
|-------|-----------|-------|
| ◯ _____ | ◯ _____ | ◯ _____ |
| ◯ _____ | ◯ _____ | ◯ _____ |
| ◯ _____ | ◯ _____ | ◯ _____ |
| ◯ _____ | ◯ _____ | ◯ _____ |
| ◯ _____ | ◯ _____ | ◯ _____ |
| ◯ _____ | ◯ _____ | ◯ _____ |
| ◯ _____ | ◯ _____ | ◯ _____ |
| ◯ _____ | ◯ _____ | ◯ _____ |

*"It only takes one person to change your life:* **YOU.** *" ~ Unknown*

## My Accomplishments this Month

| WEDNESDAY | THURSDAY | FRIDAY | SATURDAY |
|---|---|---|---|
|  |  |  |  |
|  |  |  |  |
|  |  |  |  |
|  |  |  |  |
|  |  |  |  |

### Improvements In My Life:
.
.
.
.

### Good Deeds Done:
.
.
.
.

### Fun and Spontaneous:
.
.
.
.

### I Treated Myself To:
.
.
.
.

### New Experiences:
.
.
.
.

### What made my ♥ happy this month...

_____
_____
_____
_____
_____
_____
_____

With gratitude & love, thank you.

### My Manifestation List:

| | CLAIM AS TRUE | DATE RECEIVED |
|---|---|---|
| 1. | _____ | _____ |
| 2. | _____ | _____ |
| 3. | _____ | _____ |
| 4. | _____ | _____ |
| 5. | _____ | _____ |

# $ Keeping Track of the Flow of it All

Month: _____

| DATES + DETAILS | MONEY IN | SAVINGS | SHARING WITH OTHERS | INSURANCE + HEALTH EXPENSES | HOUSE EXPENSES | GROCERIES | TRANSPORTATION EXPENSES | ENTERTAINMENT + FUN EXPENSES | HOLIDAY EXPENSES | PERSONAL EXPENSES | DINING OUT | MISC |
|---|---|---|---|---|---|---|---|---|---|---|---|---|
| | | | | | | | | | | | | |
| | | | | | | | | | | | | |
| | | | | | | | | | | | | |
| | | | | | | | | | | | | |
| | | | | | | | | | | | | |
| | | | | | | | | | | | | |
| | | | | | | | | | | | | |
| | | | | | | | | | | | | |
| | | | | | | | | | | | | |
| | | | | | | | | | | | | |
| | | | | | | | | | | | | |
| | | | | | | | | | | | | |
| | | | | | | | | | | | | |
| | | | | | | | | | | | | |
| | | | | | | | | | | | | |
| $ TOTALS | | | | | | | | | | | | |

# My Authentic Heart Words

| | | | | | |
|---|---|---|---|---|---|
| | | | | | |

| | | | | | | |
|---|---|---|---|---|---|---|
| Workout | Ⓐ Ⓒ | Ⓐ Ⓒ | Ⓐ Ⓒ | Ⓐ Ⓒ | Ⓐ Ⓒ | Ⓐ Ⓒ |
| Just for Me | ♥ | ♥ | ♥ | ♥ | ♥ | |
| Water | ⬡⬡⬡⬡⬡⬡⬡ | ⬡⬡⬡⬡⬡⬡⬡ | ⬡⬡⬡⬡⬡⬡⬡ | ⬡⬡⬡⬡⬡⬡⬡ | ⬡⬡⬡⬡⬡⬡⬡ | ⬡⬡⬡⬡⬡⬡⬡ |
| Wins ✓ | | | | | | |
| Daily Happy Moment ☺ | | | | | | |

| MONDAY ☐ | TUESDAY ☐ | WEDNESDAY ☐ | THURSDAY ☐ | FRIDAY ☐ | SATURDAY ☐ |
|---|---|---|---|---|---|
| 7:00 | 7:00 | 7:00 | 7:00 | 7:00 | |
| 8:00 | 8:00 | 8:00 | 8:00 | 8:00 | |
| 9:00 | 9:00 | 9:00 | 9:00 | 9:00 | |
| 10:00 | 10:00 | 10:00 | 10:00 | 10:00 | |
| 11:00 | 11:00 | 11:00 | 11:00 | 11:00 | |
| 12:00 | 12:00 | 12:00 | 12:00 | 12:00 | |
| 1:00 | 1:00 | 1:00 | 1:00 | 1:00 | |
| 2:00 | 2:00 | 2:00 | 2:00 | 2:00 | SUNDAY ☐ |
| 3:00 | 3:00 | 3:00 | 3:00 | 3:00 | |
| 4:00 | 4:00 | 4:00 | 4:00 | 4:00 | |
| 5:00 | 5:00 | 5:00 | 5:00 | 5:00 | |
| 6:00 | 6:00 | 6:00 | 6:00 | 6:00 | |
| 7:00 | 7:00 | 7:00 | 7:00 | 7:00 | |

| Do. Call | Do. Call | Do. Call | Do. Call | Do. Call | Do. Call |
|---|---|---|---|---|---|
| | | | | | |

| $ Money in | $ Money in | $ Money in | $ Money in | $ Money in | $ Money in |
|---|---|---|---|---|---|
| | | | | | |

## Remembering Me

I am: _____

What I love about me is: _____

_____

What I am proud of this week is: _____

_____

## Weekly Goals:

1. _____ ○  3. _____ ○

2. _____ ○  4. _____ ○

## Not to Miss:

·      ·

·      ·

## Projects to Complete:

_____
_____
_____
_____

## Recipes to Try:

_____
_____
_____
_____

## To Beautify my Home:

_____
_____
_____
_____

## Call - Email - Social Media:

·      ·

·      ·

·      ·

·      ·

## To Buy:

·      ·

·      ·

·      ·

## To Do:

_____ _____
_____ _____
_____ 

## Groceries:

_____ _____ _____
_____ _____ _____
_____ _____ _____

## My Balanced Heart

KIND KIN DEED, FAMILY HOLIDAY, COUPLES DATES, FRIENDS, HAVING FUN TOGETHER, MY FAMILY, BESTIES, SPOUSES FAMILY, KIND KID DEED, KIDS & PETS, SPOUSE, ALONE TIME, GROWING, ME, SELF CARE, MASSAGE, READING, WORK, CREATIVITY, SAVINGS, EXERCISE, SPIRITUAL WELL BEING, MUSIC, INVESTING, MEDITATION, CARDIO, WEIGHT, YOGA & STRETCHING, WALKING, CONTRIBUTING TO OTHERS, TIME IN NATURE, DEEP BREATHING

## My Weekly Reflection

## What word best describes ME this week?

# My Authentic Heart Words

| | | | | | |
|---|---|---|---|---|---|
| | | | | | |

| Workout | Ⓐ Ⓒ | Ⓐ Ⓒ | Ⓐ Ⓒ | Ⓐ Ⓒ | Ⓐ Ⓒ | Ⓐ Ⓒ |
|---|---|---|---|---|---|---|
| Just for Me | ♥ | ♥ | ♥ | ♥ | ♥ | |
| Water | ⬚⬚⬚⬚⬚⬚⬚ | ⬚⬚⬚⬚⬚⬚⬚ | ⬚⬚⬚⬚⬚⬚⬚ | ⬚⬚⬚⬚⬚⬚⬚ | ⬚⬚⬚⬚⬚⬚⬚ | ⬚⬚⬚⬚⬚⬚⬚ |
| Wins ✓ | | | | | | |
| Daily Happy Moment ☺ | | | | | | |

| MONDAY ☐ | TUESDAY ☐ | WEDNESDAY ☐ | THURSDAY ☐ | FRIDAY ☐ | SATURDAY ☐ |
|---|---|---|---|---|---|
| 7:00 | 7:00 | 7:00 | 7:00 | 7:00 | |
| 8:00 | 8:00 | 8:00 | 8:00 | 8:00 | |
| 9:00 | 9:00 | 9:00 | 9:00 | 9:00 | |
| 10:00 | 10:00 | 10:00 | 10:00 | 10:00 | |
| 11:00 | 11:00 | 11:00 | 11:00 | 11:00 | |
| 12:00 | 12:00 | 12:00 | 12:00 | 12:00 | |
| 1:00 | 1:00 | 1:00 | 1:00 | 1:00 | |
| 2:00 | 2:00 | 2:00 | 2:00 | 2:00 | SUNDAY ☐ |
| 3:00 | 3:00 | 3:00 | 3:00 | 3:00 | |
| 4:00 | 4:00 | 4:00 | 4:00 | 4:00 | |
| 5:00 | 5:00 | 5:00 | 5:00 | 5:00 | |
| 6:00 | 6:00 | 6:00 | 6:00 | 6:00 | |
| 7:00 | 7:00 | 7:00 | 7:00 | 7:00 | |

| Do. Call | Do. Call | Do. Call | Do. Call | Do. Call | Do. Call |
|---|---|---|---|---|---|
| | | | | | |

| $ Money in | $ Money in | $ Money in | $ Money in | $ Money in | $ Money in |
|---|---|---|---|---|---|
| | | | | | |

## Remembering Me

I am: _____

What I love about me is: _____

_____

What I am proud of this week is: _____

_____

## Weekly Goals:

1. _____ ◯   3. _____ ◯

2. _____ ◯   4. _____ ◯

## Not to Miss:

· _____   · _____

· _____   · _____

## Projects to Complete:

_____

_____

_____

_____

## Recipes to Try:

_____

_____

_____

_____

## To Beautify my Home:

_____

_____

_____

_____

## Call - Email - Social Media:

· _____   · _____

· _____   · _____

· _____   · _____

· _____   · _____

## To Buy:

· _____   · _____

· _____   · _____

· _____   · _____

## To Do:

_____   _____

_____   _____

_____   ## Groceries:

_____   _____   _____

_____   _____   _____

_____   _____   _____

_____   _____   _____

*My Balanced Heart*

FAMILY HOLIDAY · KIND KIN DEED · COUPLES DATES · FRIENDS · HAVING FUN TOGETHER · KIND KID DEED · MY FAMILY · BESTIES · SPOUSES FAMILY · GROWING · KIDS & PETS · SPOUSE · ALONE TIME · READING · ME · SELF CARE · MASSAGE · WORK · CREATIVITY · SAVINGS · EXERCISE · SPIRITUAL WELL BEING · MUSIC · INVESTING · CARDIO · WEIGHT · MEDITATION · YOGA & STRETCHING · WALKING · DEEP BREATHING · CONTRIBUTING TO OTHERS · TIME IN NATURE

*My Weekly Reflection*

## What word best describes ME this week?

# My Authentic Heart Words

|  |  |  |  |  |  |
|--|--|--|--|--|--|
|  |  |  |  |  |  |

| Workout | Ⓐ Ⓒ | Ⓐ Ⓒ | Ⓐ Ⓒ | Ⓐ Ⓒ | Ⓐ Ⓒ | Ⓐ Ⓒ |
|--|--|--|--|--|--|--|
| Just for Me | ♥ | ♥ | ♥ | ♥ | ♥ | |
| Water | ▭▭▭▭▭▭▭ | ▭▭▭▭▭▭▭ | ▭▭▭▭▭▭▭ | ▭▭▭▭▭▭▭ | ▭▭▭▭▭▭▭ | ▭▭▭▭▭▭▭ |
| Wins ✓ | | | | | | |
| Daily Happy Moment ☺ | | | | | | |

| MONDAY ☐ | TUESDAY ☐ | WEDNESDAY ☐ | THURSDAY ☐ | FRIDAY ☐ | SATURDAY ☐ |
|--|--|--|--|--|--|
| 7:00 | 7:00 | 7:00 | 7:00 | 7:00 | |
| 8:00 | 8:00 | 8:00 | 8:00 | 8:00 | |
| 9:00 | 9:00 | 9:00 | 9:00 | 9:00 | |
| 10:00 | 10:00 | 10:00 | 10:00 | 10:00 | |
| 11:00 | 11:00 | 11:00 | 11:00 | 11:00 | |
| 12:00 | 12:00 | 12:00 | 12:00 | 12:00 | |
| 1:00 | 1:00 | 1:00 | 1:00 | 1:00 | |
| 2:00 | 2:00 | 2:00 | 2:00 | 2:00 | SUNDAY ☐ |
| 3:00 | 3:00 | 3:00 | 3:00 | 3:00 | |
| 4:00 | 4:00 | 4:00 | 4:00 | 4:00 | |
| 5:00 | 5:00 | 5:00 | 5:00 | 5:00 | |
| 6:00 | 6:00 | 6:00 | 6:00 | 6:00 | |
| 7:00 | 7:00 | 7:00 | 7:00 | 7:00 | |

| Do. Call | Do. Call | Do. Call | Do. Call | Do. Call | Do. Call |
|--|--|--|--|--|--|
| $ Money in | $ Money in | $ Money in | $ Money in | $ Money in | $ Money in |

## Remembering Me

I am: _____

What I love about me is: _____

_____

What I am proud of this week is: _____

_____

## Weekly Goals:

1. _____ ○   3. _____ ○

2. _____ ○   4. _____ ○

## Not to Miss:

· _____   · _____

· _____   · _____

## Projects to Complete:

_____

_____

_____

_____

## Recipes to Try:

_____

_____

_____

_____

## To Beautify my Home:

_____

_____

_____

_____

## Call - Email - Social Media:

·            ·

·            ·

·            ·

·

## To Do:

_____   _____

_____   _____

_____   _____

### Groceries:

_____   _____

_____   _____

_____   _____

## To Buy:

·            ·

·            ·

·            ·

*My Balanced Heart*

FAMILY HOLIDAY
KIND KIN DEED
COUPLES DATES
FRIENDS
HAVING FUN TOGETHER
KIND KID DEED
MY FAMILY
BESTIES
SPOUSES FAMILY
KIDS & PETS
SPOUSE
GROWING
ME
ALONE TIME
SELF CARE
READING
WORK
MASSAGE
SAVINGS
EXERCISE
SPIRITUAL WELL BEING
CREATIVITY
INVESTING
MUSIC
CARDIO
MEDITATION
WEIGHT
DEEP BREATHING
YOGA & STRETCHING
WALKING
TIME IN NATURE
CONTRIBUTING TO OTHERS

*My Weekly Reflection*

## What word best describes ME this week?

# My Authentic Heart Words

| | | | | | |
|---|---|---|---|---|---|
| | | | | | |

| Workout | Ⓐ Ⓒ | Ⓐ Ⓒ | Ⓐ Ⓒ | Ⓐ Ⓒ | Ⓐ Ⓒ | Ⓐ Ⓒ |
|---|---|---|---|---|---|---|
| Just for Me | ♥ | ♥ | ♥ | ♥ | ♥ | |
| Water | ⊔⊔⊔⊔⊔⊔⊔ | ⊔⊔⊔⊔⊔⊔⊔ | ⊔⊔⊔⊔⊔⊔⊔ | ⊔⊔⊔⊔⊔⊔⊔ | ⊔⊔⊔⊔⊔⊔⊔ | ⊔⊔⊔⊔⊔⊔⊔ |
| Wins ✓ | | | | | | |
| Daily Happy Moment ☺ | | | | | | |

| MONDAY ☐ | TUESDAY ☐ | WEDNESDAY ☐ | THURSDAY ☐ | FRIDAY ☐ | SATURDAY ☐ |
|---|---|---|---|---|---|
| 7:00 | 7:00 | 7:00 | 7:00 | 7:00 | |
| 8:00 | 8:00 | 8:00 | 8:00 | 8:00 | |
| 9:00 | 9:00 | 9:00 | 9:00 | 9:00 | |
| 10:00 | 10:00 | 10:00 | 10:00 | 10:00 | |
| 11:00 | 11:00 | 11:00 | 11:00 | 11:00 | |
| 12:00 | 12:00 | 12:00 | 12:00 | 12:00 | |
| 1:00 | 1:00 | 1:00 | 1:00 | 1:00 | |
| 2:00 | 2:00 | 2:00 | 2:00 | 2:00 | SUNDAY ☐ |
| 3:00 | 3:00 | 3:00 | 3:00 | 3:00 | |
| 4:00 | 4:00 | 4:00 | 4:00 | 4:00 | |
| 5:00 | 5:00 | 5:00 | 5:00 | 5:00 | |
| 6:00 | 6:00 | 6:00 | 6:00 | 6:00 | |
| 7:00 | 7:00 | 7:00 | 7:00 | 7:00 | |

| Do. Call | Do. Call | Do. Call | Do. Call | Do. Call | Do. Call |
|---|---|---|---|---|---|
| | | | | | |

| $ Money in | $ Money in | $ Money in | $ Money in | $ Money in | $ Money in |
|---|---|---|---|---|---|
| | | | | | |

## Remembering Me

I am: _____

What I love about me is: _____

_____

What I am proud of this week is: _____

_____

## Weekly Goals:

1. _____ ○   3. _____ ○

2. _____ ○   4. _____ ○

## Not to Miss:
- .                    .
- .                    .

## Projects to Complete:

_____

_____

_____

_____

## Recipes to Try:

_____

_____

_____

_____

## To Beautify my Home:

_____

_____

_____

_____

## Call - Email - Social Media:
- .                    .
- .                    .
- .                    .
- .                    .

## To Do:

_____    _____

_____    _____

_____    

## Groceries:

_____    _____

_____    _____

## To Buy:
- .                    .
- .                    .
- .                    .

## My Balanced Heart

FAMILY HOLIDAY, KIND KIN DEED, COUPLES DATES, FRIENDS, HAVING FUN TOGETHER, MY FAMILY, BESTIES, SPOUSES FAMILY, KIND KID DEED, KIDS & PETS, SPOUSE, ALONE TIME, GROWING, ME, SELF CARE, MASSAGE, READING, WORK, CREATIVITY, SAVINGS, EXERCISE, SPIRITUAL WELL BEING, MUSIC, INVESTING, CARDIO, MEDITATION, WEIGHT, YOGA & STRETCHING, WALKING, CONTRIBUTING TO OTHERS, TIME IN NATURE, DEEP BREATHING

## My Weekly Reflection

## What word best describes ME this week?

# My Authentic Heart Words

| | | | | | |
|---|---|---|---|---|---|
| | | | | | |

| | | | | | |
|---|---|---|---|---|---|
| Workout | Ⓐ Ⓒ | Ⓐ Ⓒ | Ⓐ Ⓒ | Ⓐ Ⓒ | Ⓐ Ⓒ | Ⓐ Ⓒ |
| Just for Me | ♥ | ♥ | ♥ | ♥ | ♥ | |
| Water | ⬓⬓⬓⬓⬓⬓ | ⬓⬓⬓⬓⬓⬓ | ⬓⬓⬓⬓⬓⬓ | ⬓⬓⬓⬓⬓⬓ | ⬓⬓⬓⬓⬓⬓ | ⬓⬓⬓⬓⬓⬓ |
| Wins ✓ | | | | | | |
| Daily Happy Moment ☺ | | | | | | |

| MONDAY ☐ | TUESDAY ☐ | WEDNESDAY ☐ | THURSDAY ☐ | FRIDAY ☐ | SATURDAY ☐ |
|---|---|---|---|---|---|
| 7:00 | 7:00 | 7:00 | 7:00 | 7:00 | |
| 8:00 | 8:00 | 8:00 | 8:00 | 8:00 | |
| 9:00 | 9:00 | 9:00 | 9:00 | 9:00 | |
| 10:00 | 10:00 | 10:00 | 10:00 | 10:00 | |
| 11:00 | 11:00 | 11:00 | 11:00 | 11:00 | |
| 12:00 | 12:00 | 12:00 | 12:00 | 12:00 | |
| 1:00 | 1:00 | 1:00 | 1:00 | 1:00 | |
| 2:00 | 2:00 | 2:00 | 2:00 | 2:00 | SUNDAY ☐ |
| 3:00 | 3:00 | 3:00 | 3:00 | 3:00 | |
| 4:00 | 4:00 | 4:00 | 4:00 | 4:00 | |
| 5:00 | 5:00 | 5:00 | 5:00 | 5:00 | |
| 6:00 | 6:00 | 6:00 | 6:00 | 6:00 | |
| 7:00 | 7:00 | 7:00 | 7:00 | 7:00 | |

| Do. Call | Do. Call | Do. Call | Do. Call | Do. Call | Do. Call |
|---|---|---|---|---|---|
| | | | | | |

| $ Money in | $ Money in | $ Money in | $ Money in | $ Money in | $ Money in |
|---|---|---|---|---|---|
| | | | | | |

## Remembering Me

I am: _____

What I love about me is: _____

_____

What I am proud of this week is: _____

_____

## Weekly Goals:

1. _____ ○   3. _____ ○

2. _____ ○   4. _____ ○

## Not to Miss:

· _____     · _____

· _____     · _____

## Projects to Complete:

_____

_____

_____

_____

## Recipes to Try:

_____

_____

_____

_____

## To Beautify my Home:

_____

_____

_____

_____

## Call - Email - Social Media:

· _____     · _____

· _____     · _____

· _____     · _____

· _____     · _____

## To Do:

_____     _____

_____     _____

_____

_____     ## Groceries:

_____     _____ _____

_____     _____ _____

_____     _____ _____

## To Buy:

· _____     · _____

· _____     · _____

· _____     · _____

*My Balanced Heart*

FAMILY HOLIDAY · KIND KIN DEED · COUPLES DATES · FRIENDS · HAVING FUN TOGETHER · MY FAMILY · BESTIES · SPOUSES FAMILY · KIND KID DEED · KIDS & PETS · SPOUSE · ALONE TIME · GROWING · ME · SELF CARE · MASSAGE · READING · WORK · CREATIVITY · SAVINGS · EXERCISE · SPIRITUAL WELL BEING · MUSIC · INVESTING · MEDITATION · CARDIO · DEEP BREATHING · WEIGHT · TIME IN NATURE · YOGA & STRETCHING · WALKING · CONTRIBUTING TO OTHERS

*My Weekly Reflection*

What word best describes ME this week?

## This Month ♥

### Goals to Complete:

1. _____ ○
2. _____ ○
3. _____ ○
4. _____ ○
5. _____ ○

### Places to Explore:

_____
_____
_____
_____
_____

### To Buy:

·      · 
·      · 
·      · 

### Not to Miss:

·      · 
·      · 
·      · 

### Favorite Books I am Reading:

·      · 
·      · 

# Month: _____

| SUNDAY | MONDAY | TUESDAY |
|--------|--------|---------|
|        |        |         |
|        |        |         |
|        |        |         |
|        |        |         |
|        |        |         |

## ♥ PLAN OF ACTION

### Work:

○ _____
○ _____
○ _____
○ _____
○ _____
○ _____
○ _____
○ _____

### Personal:

○ _____
○ _____
○ _____
○ _____
○ _____
○ _____
○ _____
○ _____

### Misc:

○ _____
○ _____
○ _____
○ _____
○ _____
○ _____
○ _____
○ _____

*"Discipline is the bridge between goals and accomplishment."* ~ Jim Rohn

| WEDNESDAY | THURSDAY | FRIDAY | SATURDAY |
|---|---|---|---|
|  |  |  |  |
|  |  |  |  |
|  |  |  |  |
|  |  |  |  |
|  |  |  |  |

## What made my ♥ happy this month...

_____
_____
_____
_____
_____
_____
_____

With gratitude & love, thank you.

## My Accomplishments this Month

### Improvements In My Life:
.
.
.
.

### Good Deeds Done:
.
.
.
.

### Fun and Spontaneous:
.
.
.
.

### I Treated Myself To:
.
.
.
.

### New Experiences:
.
.
.
.

### My Manifestation List:

| | CLAIM AS TRUE | DATE RECEIVED |
|---|---|---|
| 1. | _____ | _____ |
| 2. | _____ | _____ |
| 3. | _____ | _____ |
| 4. | _____ | _____ |
| 5. | _____ | _____ |

# $ Keeping Track of the Flow of it All

Month: _____

| DATES + DETAILS | MONEY IN | SAVINGS | SHARING WITH OTHERS | INSURANCE + HEALTH EXPENSES | HOUSE EXPENSES | GROCERIES | TRANSPORTATION EXPENSES | ENTERTAINMENT + FUN EXPENSES | HOLIDAY EXPENSES | PERSONAL EXPENSES | DINING OUT | MISC |
|---|---|---|---|---|---|---|---|---|---|---|---|---|
| | | | | | | | | | | | | |
| | | | | | | | | | | | | |
| | | | | | | | | | | | | |
| | | | | | | | | | | | | |
| | | | | | | | | | | | | |
| | | | | | | | | | | | | |
| | | | | | | | | | | | | |
| | | | | | | | | | | | | |
| | | | | | | | | | | | | |
| | | | | | | | | | | | | |
| | | | | | | | | | | | | |
| | | | | | | | | | | | | |
| | | | | | | | | | | | | |
| | | | | | | | | | | | | |
| | | | | | | | | | | | | |
| $ TOTALS | | | | | | | | | | | | |

# My Authentic Heart Words

|  |  |  |  |  |  |
| --- | --- | --- | --- | --- | --- |
|  |  |  |  |  |  |

| | | | | | | |
| --- | --- | --- | --- | --- | --- | --- |
| Workout | Ⓐ Ⓒ | Ⓐ Ⓒ | Ⓐ Ⓒ | Ⓐ Ⓒ | Ⓐ Ⓒ | Ⓐ Ⓒ |
| Just for Me | ♥ | ♥ | ♥ | ♥ | ♥ | |
| Water | ⊔⊔⊔⊔⊔⊔⊔ | ⊔⊔⊔⊔⊔⊔⊔ | ⊔⊔⊔⊔⊔⊔⊔ | ⊔⊔⊔⊔⊔⊔⊔ | ⊔⊔⊔⊔⊔⊔⊔ | ⊔⊔⊔⊔⊔⊔⊔ |
| Wins ✓ | | | | | | |
| Daily Happy Moment ☺ | | | | | | |

| MONDAY ☐ | TUESDAY ☐ | WEDNESDAY ☐ | THURSDAY ☐ | FRIDAY ☐ | SATURDAY ☐ |
| --- | --- | --- | --- | --- | --- |
| 7:00 | 7:00 | 7:00 | 7:00 | 7:00 | |
| 8:00 | 8:00 | 8:00 | 8:00 | 8:00 | |
| 9:00 | 9:00 | 9:00 | 9:00 | 9:00 | |
| 10:00 | 10:00 | 10:00 | 10:00 | 10:00 | |
| 11:00 | 11:00 | 11:00 | 11:00 | 11:00 | |
| 12:00 | 12:00 | 12:00 | 12:00 | 12:00 | |
| 1:00 | 1:00 | 1:00 | 1:00 | 1:00 | |
| 2:00 | 2:00 | 2:00 | 2:00 | 2:00 | SUNDAY ☐ |
| 3:00 | 3:00 | 3:00 | 3:00 | 3:00 | |
| 4:00 | 4:00 | 4:00 | 4:00 | 4:00 | |
| 5:00 | 5:00 | 5:00 | 5:00 | 5:00 | |
| 6:00 | 6:00 | 6:00 | 6:00 | 6:00 | |
| 7:00 | 7:00 | 7:00 | 7:00 | 7:00 | |

| Do. Call | Do. Call | Do. Call | Do. Call | Do. Call | Do. Call |
| --- | --- | --- | --- | --- | --- |
| | | | | | |

| $ Money in | $ Money in | $ Money in | $ Money in | $ Money in | $ Money in |
| --- | --- | --- | --- | --- | --- |
| | | | | | |

## Remembering Me

I am: _____

What I love about me is: _____

_____

What I am proud of this week is: _____

## Weekly Goals:

1. _____ ○   3. _____ ○

2. _____ ○   4. _____ ○

## Not to Miss:

· 

· 

· 

· 

## Projects to Complete:

_____

_____

_____

_____

## Recipes to Try:

_____

_____

_____

_____

## To Beautify my Home:

_____

_____

_____

_____

## Call - Email - Social Media:

· 

· 

· 

· 

· 

· 

· 

· 

## To Do:

_____

_____

_____

_____

_____

_____

### Groceries:

_____ _____

_____ _____

_____ _____

_____ _____

## To Buy:

· 

· 

· 

· 

· 

· 

*My Balanced Heart*

*My Weekly Reflection*

What word best describes ME this week?

| | | | | | |
|---|---|---|---|---|---|
| | | | | | |

| | | | | | | |
|---|---|---|---|---|---|---|
| Workout | Ⓐ Ⓒ | Ⓐ Ⓒ | Ⓐ Ⓒ | Ⓐ Ⓒ | Ⓐ Ⓒ | Ⓐ Ⓒ |
| Just for Me | ♥ | ♥ | ♥ | ♥ | ♥ | |
| Water | 🥛🥛🥛🥛🥛🥛 | 🥛🥛🥛🥛🥛🥛 | 🥛🥛🥛🥛🥛🥛 | 🥛🥛🥛🥛🥛🥛 | 🥛🥛🥛🥛🥛🥛 | 🥛🥛🥛🥛🥛🥛 |
| Wins ✓ | | | | | | |
| Daily Happy Moment ☺ | | | | | | |

| MONDAY ☐ | TUESDAY ☐ | WEDNESDAY ☐ | THURSDAY ☐ | FRIDAY ☐ | SATURDAY ☐ |
|---|---|---|---|---|---|
| 7:00 | 7:00 | 7:00 | 7:00 | 7:00 | |
| 8:00 | 8:00 | 8:00 | 8:00 | 8:00 | |
| 9:00 | 9:00 | 9:00 | 9:00 | 9:00 | |
| 10:00 | 10:00 | 10:00 | 10:00 | 10:00 | |
| 11:00 | 11:00 | 11:00 | 11:00 | 11:00 | |
| 12:00 | 12:00 | 12:00 | 12:00 | 12:00 | |
| 1:00 | 1:00 | 1:00 | 1:00 | 1:00 | |
| 2:00 | 2:00 | 2:00 | 2:00 | 2:00 | SUNDAY ☐ |
| 3:00 | 3:00 | 3:00 | 3:00 | 3:00 | |
| 4:00 | 4:00 | 4:00 | 4:00 | 4:00 | |
| 5:00 | 5:00 | 5:00 | 5:00 | 5:00 | |
| 6:00 | 6:00 | 6:00 | 6:00 | 6:00 | |
| 7:00 | 7:00 | 7:00 | 7:00 | 7:00 | |

| Do. Call | Do. Call | Do. Call | Do. Call | Do. Call | Do. Call |
|---|---|---|---|---|---|
| | | | | | |

| $ Money in | $ Money in | $ Money in | $ Money in | $ Money in | $ Money in |
|---|---|---|---|---|---|
| | | | | | |

## Remembering Me

I am: _____

What I love about me is: _____

_____

What I am proud of this week is: _____

_____

## Weekly Goals:

1. _____ ○     3. _____ ○

2. _____ ○     4. _____ ○

## Not to Miss:

· _____     · _____

· _____     · _____

## Projects to Complete:

_____

_____

_____

_____

## Recipes to Try:

_____

_____

_____

_____

## To Beautify my Home:

_____

_____

_____

_____

## Call - Email - Social Media:

· _____     · _____

· _____     · _____

· _____     · _____

· _____     · _____

## To Do:

_____

_____

_____

_____

_____

## Groceries:

_____  _____

_____  _____

_____  _____

_____  _____

## To Buy:

· _____     · _____

· _____     · _____

## My Balanced Heart

COUPLES DATES, FRIENDS, HAVING FUN TOGETHER, SPOUSES FAMILY, SPOUSE, ALONE TIME, SELF CARE, MASSAGE, CREATIVITY, MUSIC, MEDITATION, DEEP BREATHING, TIME IN NATURE, CONTRIBUTING TO OTHERS, WALKING, YOGA & STRETCHING, WEIGHT, CARDIO, INVESTING, SAVINGS, READING, GROWING, KIND KID DEED, FAMILY HOLIDAY, KIND KIN DEED

MY FAMILY, BESTIES, KIDS & PETS, SPOUSE, WORK, EXERCISE, SPIRITUAL WELL BEING, ME

## My Weekly Reflection

## What word best describes ME this week?

161

# My Authentic Heart Words

| | | | | | |
|---|---|---|---|---|---|
| | | | | | |

| Workout | Ⓐ Ⓒ | Ⓐ Ⓒ | Ⓐ Ⓒ | Ⓐ Ⓒ | Ⓐ Ⓒ | Ⓐ Ⓒ |
|---|---|---|---|---|---|---|
| Just for Me | ♥ | ♥ | ♥ | ♥ | ♥ | |
| Water | ⬚⬚⬚⬚⬚⬚⬚ | ⬚⬚⬚⬚⬚⬚⬚ | ⬚⬚⬚⬚⬚⬚⬚ | ⬚⬚⬚⬚⬚⬚⬚ | ⬚⬚⬚⬚⬚⬚⬚ | ⬚⬚⬚⬚⬚⬚⬚ |
| Wins ✓ | | | | | | |
| Daily Happy Moment ☺ | | | | | | |

| MONDAY ☐ | TUESDAY ☐ | WEDNESDAY ☐ | THURSDAY ☐ | FRIDAY ☐ | SATURDAY ☐ |
|---|---|---|---|---|---|
| 7:00 | 7:00 | 7:00 | 7:00 | 7:00 | |
| 8:00 | 8:00 | 8:00 | 8:00 | 8:00 | |
| 9:00 | 9:00 | 9:00 | 9:00 | 9:00 | |
| 10:00 | 10:00 | 10:00 | 10:00 | 10:00 | |
| 11:00 | 11:00 | 11:00 | 11:00 | 11:00 | |
| 12:00 | 12:00 | 12:00 | 12:00 | 12:00 | |
| 1:00 | 1:00 | 1:00 | 1:00 | 1:00 | |
| 2:00 | 2:00 | 2:00 | 2:00 | 2:00 | SUNDAY ☐ |
| 3:00 | 3:00 | 3:00 | 3:00 | 3:00 | |
| 4:00 | 4:00 | 4:00 | 4:00 | 4:00 | |
| 5:00 | 5:00 | 5:00 | 5:00 | 5:00 | |
| 6:00 | 6:00 | 6:00 | 6:00 | 6:00 | |
| 7:00 | 7:00 | 7:00 | 7:00 | 7:00 | |

| Do. Call | Do. Call | Do. Call | Do. Call | Do. Call | Do. Call |
|---|---|---|---|---|---|
| | | | | | |

| $ Money in | $ Money in | $ Money in | $ Money in | $ Money in | $ Money in |
|---|---|---|---|---|---|
| | | | | | |

## Remembering Me

I am: _____

What I love about me is: _____

_____

What I am proud of this week is: _____

_____

## Weekly Goals:

1. _____ ○   3. _____ ○

2. _____ ○   4. _____ ○

## Not to Miss:

· 

· 

## Projects to Complete:

_____

_____

_____

_____

## Recipes to Try:

_____

_____

_____

_____

## To Beautify my Home:

_____

_____

_____

_____

## Call - Email - Social Media:

·      ·

·      ·

·      ·

·      ·

## To Do:

_____   _____

_____   _____

_____

### Groceries:

_____   _____   _____

_____   _____   _____

_____   _____   _____

_____   _____   _____

## To Buy:

·      ·

·      ·

·      ·

## My Balanced Heart

KIND KIN DEED · FAMILY HOLIDAY · COUPLES DATES · FRIENDS · HAVING FUN TOGETHER · MY FAMILY · BESTIES · SPOUSES FAMILY · KIND KID DEED · KIDS & PETS · SPOUSE · GROWING · ME · ALONE TIME · READING · WORK · SELF CARE · MASSAGE · SAVINGS · EXERCISE · SPIRITUAL WELL BEING · CREATIVITY · INVESTING · MUSIC · CARDIO · MEDITATION · WEIGHT · YOGA & STRETCHING · WALKING · DEEP BREATHING · CONTRIBUTING TO OTHERS · TIME IN NATURE

## My Weekly Reflection

## What word best describes ME this week?

# My Authentic Heart Words

| | | | | | |
|---|---|---|---|---|---|
| | | | | | |

| | | | | | | |
|---|---|---|---|---|---|---|
| Workout | Ⓐ Ⓒ | Ⓐ Ⓒ | Ⓐ Ⓒ | Ⓐ Ⓒ | Ⓐ Ⓒ | Ⓐ Ⓒ |
| Just for Me | ♥ | ♥ | ♥ | ♥ | ♥ | |
| Water | ⬜⬜⬜⬜⬜⬜⬜ | ⬜⬜⬜⬜⬜⬜⬜ | ⬜⬜⬜⬜⬜⬜⬜ | ⬜⬜⬜⬜⬜⬜⬜ | ⬜⬜⬜⬜⬜⬜⬜ | ⬜⬜⬜⬜⬜⬜⬜ |
| Wins ✓ | | | | | | |
| Daily Happy Moment ☺ | | | | | | |

| MONDAY ☐ | TUESDAY ☐ | WEDNESDAY ☐ | THURSDAY ☐ | FRIDAY ☐ | SATURDAY ☐ |
|---|---|---|---|---|---|
| 7:00 | 7:00 | 7:00 | 7:00 | 7:00 | |
| 8:00 | 8:00 | 8:00 | 8:00 | 8:00 | |
| 9:00 | 9:00 | 9:00 | 9:00 | 9:00 | |
| 10:00 | 10:00 | 10:00 | 10:00 | 10:00 | |
| 11:00 | 11:00 | 11:00 | 11:00 | 11:00 | |
| 12:00 | 12:00 | 12:00 | 12:00 | 12:00 | |
| 1:00 | 1:00 | 1:00 | 1:00 | 1:00 | |
| 2:00 | 2:00 | 2:00 | 2:00 | 2:00 | SUNDAY ☐ |
| 3:00 | 3:00 | 3:00 | 3:00 | 3:00 | |
| 4:00 | 4:00 | 4:00 | 4:00 | 4:00 | |
| 5:00 | 5:00 | 5:00 | 5:00 | 5:00 | |
| 6:00 | 6:00 | 6:00 | 6:00 | 6:00 | |
| 7:00 | 7:00 | 7:00 | 7:00 | 7:00 | |

| Do. Call | Do. Call | Do. Call | Do. Call | Do. Call | Do. Call |
|---|---|---|---|---|---|
| _____ | _____ | _____ | _____ | _____ | _____ |
| _____ | _____ | _____ | _____ | _____ | _____ |
| _____ | _____ | _____ | _____ | _____ | _____ |
| _____ | _____ | _____ | _____ | _____ | _____ |
| _____ | _____ | _____ | _____ | _____ | _____ |
| _____ | _____ | _____ | _____ | _____ | _____ |
| _____ | _____ | _____ | _____ | _____ | _____ |
| _____ | _____ | _____ | _____ | _____ | _____ |
| $ Money in | $ Money in | $ Money in | $ Money in | $ Money in | $ Money in |
| _____ | _____ | _____ | _____ | _____ | _____ |
| _____ | _____ | _____ | _____ | _____ | _____ |

## Remembering Me

I am: _____

What I love about me is: _____

_____

What I am proud of this week is: _____

_____

## Weekly Goals:

1. _____ ○    3. _____ ○

2. _____ ○    4. _____ ○

## Not to Miss:

.         .

.         .

## Projects to Complete:

_____

_____

_____

_____

## Recipes to Try:

_____

_____

_____

_____

## To Beautify my Home:

_____

_____

_____

_____

## Call - Email - Social Media:

.         .

.         .

.         .

.         .

## To Do:

_____

_____

_____

## Groceries:

_____

_____

_____

_____

## To Buy:

.         .

.         .

.         .

*My Balanced Heart*

FAMILY HOLIDAY · KIND KIN DEED · COUPLES DATES · FRIENDS · HAVING FUN TOGETHER · KIND KID DEED · MY FAMILY · BESTIES · SPOUSES FAMILY · KIDS & PETS · SPOUSE · ALONE TIME · GROWING · ME · SELF CARE · MASSAGE · READING · WORK · CREATIVITY · SAVINGS · EXERCISE · SPIRITUAL WELL BEING · MUSIC · INVESTING · CARDIO · MEDITATION · WEIGHT · DEEP BREATHING · YOGA & STRETCHING · WALKING · CONTRIBUTING TO OTHERS · TIME IN NATURE

*My Weekly Reflection*

## What word best describes ME this week?

# My Authentic Heart Words

| | | | | | |
|---|---|---|---|---|---|
| | | | | | |

| Workout | Ⓐ Ⓒ | Ⓐ Ⓒ | Ⓐ Ⓒ | Ⓐ Ⓒ | Ⓐ Ⓒ | Ⓐ Ⓒ |
|---|---|---|---|---|---|---|
| Just for Me | ♥ | ♥ | ♥ | ♥ | ♥ | |
| Water | ▢▢▢▢▢▢▢ | ▢▢▢▢▢▢▢ | ▢▢▢▢▢▢▢ | ▢▢▢▢▢▢▢ | ▢▢▢▢▢▢▢ | ▢▢▢▢▢▢▢ |
| Wins ✓ | | | | | | |
| Daily Happy Moment ☺ | | | | | | |

| MONDAY ☐ | TUESDAY ☐ | WEDNESDAY ☐ | THURSDAY ☐ | FRIDAY ☐ | SATURDAY ☐ |
|---|---|---|---|---|---|
| 7:00 | 7:00 | 7:00 | 7:00 | 7:00 | |
| 8:00 | 8:00 | 8:00 | 8:00 | 8:00 | |
| 9:00 | 9:00 | 9:00 | 9:00 | 9:00 | |
| 10:00 | 10:00 | 10:00 | 10:00 | 10:00 | |
| 11:00 | 11:00 | 11:00 | 11:00 | 11:00 | |
| 12:00 | 12:00 | 12:00 | 12:00 | 12:00 | |
| 1:00 | 1:00 | 1:00 | 1:00 | 1:00 | |
| 2:00 | 2:00 | 2:00 | 2:00 | 2:00 | SUNDAY ☐ |
| 3:00 | 3:00 | 3:00 | 3:00 | 3:00 | |
| 4:00 | 4:00 | 4:00 | 4:00 | 4:00 | |
| 5:00 | 5:00 | 5:00 | 5:00 | 5:00 | |
| 6:00 | 6:00 | 6:00 | 6:00 | 6:00 | |
| 7:00 | 7:00 | 7:00 | 7:00 | 7:00 | |

| Do. Call | Do. Call | Do. Call | Do. Call | Do. Call | Do. Call |
|---|---|---|---|---|---|
| | | | | | |

| $ Money in | $ Money in | $ Money in | $ Money in | $ Money in | $ Money in |
|---|---|---|---|---|---|
| | | | | | |

## Remembering Me

I am: _____

What I love about me is: _____

_____

What I am proud of this week is: _____

_____

## Weekly Goals:

1. _____ ○   3. _____ ○

2. _____ ○   4. _____ ○

## Not to Miss:

· _____   · _____

· _____   · _____

## Projects to Complete:

_____

_____

_____

_____

## Recipes to Try:

_____

_____

_____

_____

## To Beautify my Home:

_____

_____

_____

_____

## Call - Email - Social Media:

· _____   · _____

· _____   · _____

· _____   · _____

· _____   · _____

## To Buy:

· _____   · _____

· _____   · _____

· _____   · _____

## To Do:

_____

_____

_____

### Groceries:

_____

_____

_____

_____

_____

*My Balanced Heart*

FAMILY HOLIDAY · KIND KIN DEED · COUPLES DATES · FRIENDS · HAVING FUN TOGETHER · KIND KID DEED · MY FAMILY · BESTIES · SPOUSES FAMILY · GROWING · KIDS & PETS · SPOUSE · ALONE TIME · READING · ME · SELF CARE · MASSAGE · WORK · CREATIVITY · SAVINGS · EXERCISE · SPIRITUAL WELL BEING · MUSIC · INVESTING · CARDIO · MEDITATION · WEIGHT · DEEP BREATHING · YOGA & STRETCHING · WALKING · TIME IN NATURE · CONTRIBUTING TO OTHERS

*My Weekly Reflection*

## What word best describes ME this week?

**This Month ♥**

### Goals to Complete:

1. _____ ○
2. _____ ○
3. _____ ○
4. _____ ○
5. _____ ○

### Places to Explore:

_____
_____
_____
_____
_____

### To Buy:

- ·          ·
- ·          ·
- ·          ·

### Not to Miss:

- ·          ·
- ·          ·
- ·          ·

### Favorite Books I am Reading:

- ·          ·
- ·          ·

| SUNDAY | MONDAY | TUESDAY |
|---|---|---|
| | | |
| | | |
| | | |
| | | |
| | | |

### ♥ PLAN OF ACTION

**Work:**

○ _____
○ _____
○ _____
○ _____
○ _____
○ _____
○ _____
○ _____

**Personal:**

○ _____
○ _____
○ _____
○ _____
○ _____
○ _____
○ _____
○ _____

**Misc:**

○ _____
○ _____
○ _____
○ _____
○ _____
○ _____
○ _____
○ _____

*"Happiness is when what you think, what you say, and what you do are in harmony." ~ Gandhi*

| WEDNESDAY | THURSDAY | FRIDAY | SATURDAY |
|---|---|---|---|
|  |  |  |  |
|  |  |  |  |
|  |  |  |  |
|  |  |  |  |
|  |  |  |  |

## My Accomplishments this Month

### Improvements In My Life:
·
·
·
·

### Good Deeds Done:
·
·
·
·

### Fun and Spontaneous:
·
·
·
·

### I Treated Myself To:
·
·
·
·

### New Experiences:
·
·
·
·

### My Manifestation List:

| | CLAIM AS TRUE | DATE RECEIVED |
|---|---|---|
| 1. | _____ | _____ |
| 2. | _____ | _____ |
| 3. | _____ | _____ |
| 4. | _____ | _____ |
| 5. | _____ | _____ |

## What made my ♥ happy this month...

_____
_____
_____
_____
_____
_____
_____

With gratitude & love, thank you.

# $ Keeping Track of the Flow of it All

**Month:** _____

| DATES + DETAILS | MONEY IN | SAVINGS | SHARING WITH OTHERS | INSURANCE + HEALTH EXPENSES | HOUSE EXPENSES | GROCERIES | TRANSPORTATION EXPENSES | ENTERTAINMENT + FUN EXPENSES | HOLIDAY EXPENSES | PERSONAL EXPENSES | DINING OUT | MISC |
|---|---|---|---|---|---|---|---|---|---|---|---|---|
| | | | | | | | | | | | | |
| | | | | | | | | | | | | |
| | | | | | | | | | | | | |
| | | | | | | | | | | | | |
| | | | | | | | | | | | | |
| | | | | | | | | | | | | |
| | | | | | | | | | | | | |
| | | | | | | | | | | | | |
| | | | | | | | | | | | | |
| | | | | | | | | | | | | |
| | | | | | | | | | | | | |
| | | | | | | | | | | | | |
| | | | | | | | | | | | | |
| | | | | | | | | | | | | |
| | | | | | | | | | | | | |
| | | | | | | | | | | | | |
| $ TOTALS | | | | | | | | | | | | |

# My Journaling Space ♥

# My Authentic Heart Words

| | | | | | |
|---|---|---|---|---|---|
| | | | | | |

| | | | | | | |
|---|---|---|---|---|---|---|
| Workout | Ⓐ Ⓒ | Ⓐ Ⓒ | Ⓐ Ⓒ | Ⓐ Ⓒ | Ⓐ Ⓒ | Ⓐ Ⓒ |
| Just for Me | ♥ | ♥ | ♥ | ♥ | ♥ | |
| Water | ⬜⬜⬜⬜⬜⬜⬜ | ⬜⬜⬜⬜⬜⬜⬜ | ⬜⬜⬜⬜⬜⬜⬜ | ⬜⬜⬜⬜⬜⬜⬜ | ⬜⬜⬜⬜⬜⬜⬜ | ⬜⬜⬜⬜⬜⬜⬜ |
| Wins ✓ | | | | | | |
| Daily Happy Moment ☺ | | | | | | |

| MONDAY ☐ | TUESDAY ☐ | WEDNESDAY ☐ | THURSDAY ☐ | FRIDAY ☐ | SATURDAY ☐ |
|---|---|---|---|---|---|
| 7:00 | 7:00 | 7:00 | 7:00 | 7:00 | |
| 8:00 | 8:00 | 8:00 | 8:00 | 8:00 | |
| 9:00 | 9:00 | 9:00 | 9:00 | 9:00 | |
| 10:00 | 10:00 | 10:00 | 10:00 | 10:00 | |
| 11:00 | 11:00 | 11:00 | 11:00 | 11:00 | |
| 12:00 | 12:00 | 12:00 | 12:00 | 12:00 | |
| 1:00 | 1:00 | 1:00 | 1:00 | 1:00 | |
| 2:00 | 2:00 | 2:00 | 2:00 | 2:00 | SUNDAY ☐ |
| 3:00 | 3:00 | 3:00 | 3:00 | 3:00 | |
| 4:00 | 4:00 | 4:00 | 4:00 | 4:00 | |
| 5:00 | 5:00 | 5:00 | 5:00 | 5:00 | |
| 6:00 | 6:00 | 6:00 | 6:00 | 6:00 | |
| 7:00 | 7:00 | 7:00 | 7:00 | 7:00 | |

| Do. Call | Do. Call | Do. Call | Do. Call | Do. Call | Do. Call |
|---|---|---|---|---|---|
| | | | | | |

| $ Money in | $ Money in | $ Money in | $ Money in | $ Money in | $ Money in |
|---|---|---|---|---|---|
| | | | | | |

172

## Remembering Me

I am: _____

What I love about me is: _____

_____

What I am proud of this week is: _____

_____

## Weekly Goals:

1. _____ ○   3. _____ ○

2. _____ ○   4. _____ ○

## Not to Miss:

· _____   · _____

· _____   · _____

## Projects to Complete:

_____

_____

_____

_____

## Recipes to Try:

_____

_____

_____

_____

## To Beautify my Home:

_____

_____

_____

_____

## Call - Email - Social Media:

· _____   · _____

· _____   · _____

· _____   · _____

· _____   · _____

## To Do:

_____   _____

_____   _____

_____

## Groceries:

_____   _____

_____   _____

## To Buy:

· _____   · _____

· _____   · _____

· _____   · _____

*My Balanced Heart*

FAMILY HOLIDAY
KIND KIN DEED
COUPLES DATES
FRIENDS
HAVING FUN TOGETHER
MY FAMILY
BESTIES
SPOUSES FAMILY
KIND KID DEED
KIDS & PETS
SPOUSE
GROWING
ME
ALONE TIME
SELF CARE
READING
WORK
MASSAGE
SAVINGS
EXERCISE
SPIRITUAL WELL BEING
CREATIVITY
INVESTING
MUSIC
CARDIO
MEDITATION
WEIGHT
DEEP BREATHING
YOGA & STRETCHING
WALKING
TIME IN NATURE
CONTRIBUTING TO OTHERS

*My Weekly Reflection*

## What word best describes ME this week?

# My Authentic Heart Words

| | | | | | |
|---|---|---|---|---|---|
| Workout | Ⓐ Ⓒ | Ⓐ Ⓒ | Ⓐ Ⓒ | Ⓐ Ⓒ | Ⓐ Ⓒ | Ⓐ Ⓒ |

| | | | | | |
|---|---|---|---|---|---|
| Just for Me | ♥ | ♥ | ♥ | ♥ | ♥ | |

Water

Wins ✓

Daily Happy Moment ☺

| MONDAY ☐ | TUESDAY ☐ | WEDNESDAY ☐ | THURSDAY ☐ | FRIDAY ☐ | SATURDAY ☐ |
|---|---|---|---|---|---|
| 7:00 | 7:00 | 7:00 | 7:00 | 7:00 | |
| 8:00 | 8:00 | 8:00 | 8:00 | 8:00 | |
| 9:00 | 9:00 | 9:00 | 9:00 | 9:00 | |
| 10:00 | 10:00 | 10:00 | 10:00 | 10:00 | |
| 11:00 | 11:00 | 11:00 | 11:00 | 11:00 | |
| 12:00 | 12:00 | 12:00 | 12:00 | 12:00 | |
| 1:00 | 1:00 | 1:00 | 1:00 | 1:00 | |
| 2:00 | 2:00 | 2:00 | 2:00 | 2:00 | SUNDAY ☐ |
| 3:00 | 3:00 | 3:00 | 3:00 | 3:00 | |
| 4:00 | 4:00 | 4:00 | 4:00 | 4:00 | |
| 5:00 | 5:00 | 5:00 | 5:00 | 5:00 | |
| 6:00 | 6:00 | 6:00 | 6:00 | 6:00 | |
| 7:00 | 7:00 | 7:00 | 7:00 | 7:00 | |

| Do. Call | Do. Call | Do. Call | Do. Call | Do. Call | Do. Call |
|---|---|---|---|---|---|

| $ Money in | $ Money in | $ Money in | $ Money in | $ Money in | $ Money in |
|---|---|---|---|---|---|

## Remembering Me

I am: _____

What I love about me is: _____

_____

What I am proud of this week is: _____

_____

## Weekly Goals:

1. _____ ○  3. _____ ○

2. _____ ○  4. _____ ○

## Not to Miss:

· _____  · _____

· _____  · _____

## Projects to Complete:

_____

_____

_____

_____

## Recipes to Try:

_____

_____

_____

_____

## To Beautify my Home:

_____

_____

_____

_____

## Call - Email - Social Media:

· _____  · _____

· _____  · _____

· _____  · _____

· _____  · _____

## To Do:

_____

_____

_____

_____

_____

_____

### Groceries:

_____ _____

_____ _____

_____ _____

_____ _____

## To Buy:

· _____  · _____

· _____  · _____

· _____  · _____

## My Balanced Heart

KIND KIN DEED
FAMILY HOLIDAY
COUPLES DATES
FRIENDS
HAVING FUN TOGETHER
KIND KID DEED
MY FAMILY
BESTIES
SPOUSES FAMILY
GROWING
KIDS & PETS
SPOUSE
ALONE TIME
READING
ME
WORK
SELF CARE
MASSAGE
SAVINGS
EXERCISE
SPIRITUAL WELL BEING
CREATIVITY
INVESTING
MUSIC
CARDIO
MEDITATION
WEIGHT
DEEP BREATHING
YOGA & STRETCHING
WALKING
TIME IN NATURE
CONTRIBUTING TO OTHERS

## My Weekly Reflection

## What word best describes ME this week?

# My Authentic Heart Words

| | | | | | |
|---|---|---|---|---|---|
| | | | | | |

| | | | | | | |
|---|---|---|---|---|---|---|
| Workout | Ⓐ Ⓒ | Ⓐ Ⓒ | Ⓐ Ⓒ | Ⓐ Ⓒ | Ⓐ Ⓒ | Ⓐ Ⓒ |
| Just for Me | ♥ | ♥ | ♥ | ♥ | ♥ | |
| Water | ⬚⬚⬚⬚⬚⬚⬚ | ⬚⬚⬚⬚⬚⬚⬚ | ⬚⬚⬚⬚⬚⬚⬚ | ⬚⬚⬚⬚⬚⬚⬚ | ⬚⬚⬚⬚⬚⬚⬚ | ⬚⬚⬚⬚⬚⬚⬚ |
| Wins ✓ | | | | | | |
| Daily Happy Moment ☺ | | | | | | |

| MONDAY ☐ | TUESDAY ☐ | WEDNESDAY ☐ | THURSDAY ☐ | FRIDAY ☐ | SATURDAY ☐ |
|---|---|---|---|---|---|
| 7:00 | 7:00 | 7:00 | 7:00 | 7:00 | |
| 8:00 | 8:00 | 8:00 | 8:00 | 8:00 | |
| 9:00 | 9:00 | 9:00 | 9:00 | 9:00 | |
| 10:00 | 10:00 | 10:00 | 10:00 | 10:00 | |
| 11:00 | 11:00 | 11:00 | 11:00 | 11:00 | |
| 12:00 | 12:00 | 12:00 | 12:00 | 12:00 | |
| 1:00 | 1:00 | 1:00 | 1:00 | 1:00 | |
| 2:00 | 2:00 | 2:00 | 2:00 | 2:00 | SUNDAY ☐ |
| 3:00 | 3:00 | 3:00 | 3:00 | 3:00 | |
| 4:00 | 4:00 | 4:00 | 4:00 | 4:00 | |
| 5:00 | 5:00 | 5:00 | 5:00 | 5:00 | |
| 6:00 | 6:00 | 6:00 | 6:00 | 6:00 | |
| 7:00 | 7:00 | 7:00 | 7:00 | 7:00 | |

| Do. Call | Do. Call | Do. Call | Do. Call | Do. Call | Do. Call |
|---|---|---|---|---|---|
| | | | | | |

| $ Money in | $ Money in | $ Money in | $ Money in | $ Money in | $ Money in |
|---|---|---|---|---|---|
| | | | | | |

## Remembering Me

I am: _____

What I love about me is: _____

_____

What I am proud of this week is: _____

_____

## Weekly Goals:

1. _____ ○   3. _____ ○

2. _____ ○   4. _____ ○

## Not to Miss:

· _____      · _____

· _____      · _____

## Projects to Complete:

_____

_____

_____

_____

## Recipes to Try:

_____

_____

_____

_____

## To Beautify my Home:

_____

_____

_____

_____

## Call - Email - Social Media:

· _____   · _____

· _____   · _____

· _____   · _____

· _____   · _____

## To Buy:

· _____   · _____

· _____   · _____

· _____   · _____

## To Do:

_____   _____

_____   _____

_____   _____

## Groceries:

_____   _____

_____   _____

_____   _____

_____   _____

## My Balanced Heart

COUPLES DATES
FRIENDS
HAVING FUN TOGETHER
SPOUSES FAMILY
ALONE TIME
MASSAGE
CREATIVITY
MUSIC
MEDITATION
DEEP BREATHING
TIME IN NATURE
CONTRIBUTING TO OTHERS
WALKING
YOGA & STRETCHING
WEIGHT
CARDIO
INVESTING
SAVINGS
READING
GROWING
KIND KID DEED
FAMILY HOLIDAY
KIND KIN DEED
MY FAMILY
BESTIES
KIDS & PETS
SPOUSE
ME
SELF CARE
WORK
EXERCISE
SPIRITUAL WELL BEING

## My Weekly Reflection

## What word best describes ME this week?

# My Authentic Heart Words

| | | | | | |
|---|---|---|---|---|---|
| Workout Ⓐ Ⓒ | Ⓐ Ⓒ | Ⓐ Ⓒ | Ⓐ Ⓒ | Ⓐ Ⓒ | Ⓐ Ⓒ |
| Just for Me | ♥ | ♥ | ♥ | ♥ | ♥ |
| Water | ⊔⊔⊔⊔⊔⊔⊔ | ⊔⊔⊔⊔⊔⊔⊔ | ⊔⊔⊔⊔⊔⊔⊔ | ⊔⊔⊔⊔⊔⊔⊔ | ⊔⊔⊔⊔⊔⊔⊔ |
| Wins ✓ | | | | | |
| Daily Happy Moment ☺ | | | | | |

| MONDAY ☐ | TUESDAY ☐ | WEDNESDAY ☐ | THURSDAY ☐ | FRIDAY ☐ | SATURDAY ☐ |
|---|---|---|---|---|---|
| 7:00 | 7:00 | 7:00 | 7:00 | 7:00 | |
| 8:00 | 8:00 | 8:00 | 8:00 | 8:00 | |
| 9:00 | 9:00 | 9:00 | 9:00 | 9:00 | |
| 10:00 | 10:00 | 10:00 | 10:00 | 10:00 | |
| 11:00 | 11:00 | 11:00 | 11:00 | 11:00 | |
| 12:00 | 12:00 | 12:00 | 12:00 | 12:00 | |
| 1:00 | 1:00 | 1:00 | 1:00 | 1:00 | |
| 2:00 | 2:00 | 2:00 | 2:00 | 2:00 | SUNDAY ☐ |
| 3:00 | 3:00 | 3:00 | 3:00 | 3:00 | |
| 4:00 | 4:00 | 4:00 | 4:00 | 4:00 | |
| 5:00 | 5:00 | 5:00 | 5:00 | 5:00 | |
| 6:00 | 6:00 | 6:00 | 6:00 | 6:00 | |
| 7:00 | 7:00 | 7:00 | 7:00 | 7:00 | |

| Do. Call | Do. Call | Do. Call | Do. Call | Do. Call | Do. Call |
|---|---|---|---|---|---|
| | | | | | |

| $ Money in | $ Money in | $ Money in | $ Money in | $ Money in | $ Money in |
|---|---|---|---|---|---|
| | | | | | |

## Remembering Me

I am: _____

What I love about me is: _____

_____

What I am proud of this week is: _____

_____

## Weekly Goals:

1. _____ ○   3. _____ ○

2. _____ ○   4. _____ ○

## Not to Miss:

- .                    .
- .                    .

## Projects to Complete:

_____

_____

_____

## Recipes to Try:

_____

_____

_____

## To Beautify my Home:

_____

_____

_____

## Call - Email - Social Media:

- .          .
- .          .
- .          .
- .          .

## To Do:

_____   _____

_____   _____

_____

### Groceries:

_____   _____   _____

_____   _____   _____

## To Buy:

- .          .
- .          .
- .          .

_____   _____   _____

_____   _____   _____

_____   _____   _____

### My Balanced Heart

### My Weekly Reflection

### What word best describes ME this week?

179

# My Authentic Heart Words

|  |  |  |  |  |  |
|---|---|---|---|---|---|
|  |  |  |  |  |  |

| | | | | | |
|---|---|---|---|---|---|
| Workout | Ⓐ Ⓒ | Ⓐ Ⓒ | Ⓐ Ⓒ | Ⓐ Ⓒ | Ⓐ Ⓒ | Ⓐ Ⓒ |
| Just for Me | ♥ | ♥ | ♥ | ♥ | ♥ | |
| Water | | | | | | |
| Wins ✓ | | | | | | |
| Daily Happy Moment ☺ | | | | | | |

| MONDAY ☐ | TUESDAY ☐ | WEDNESDAY ☐ | THURSDAY ☐ | FRIDAY ☐ | SATURDAY ☐ |
|---|---|---|---|---|---|
| 7:00 | 7:00 | 7:00 | 7:00 | 7:00 | |
| 8:00 | 8:00 | 8:00 | 8:00 | 8:00 | |
| 9:00 | 9:00 | 9:00 | 9:00 | 9:00 | |
| 10:00 | 10:00 | 10:00 | 10:00 | 10:00 | |
| 11:00 | 11:00 | 11:00 | 11:00 | 11:00 | |
| 12:00 | 12:00 | 12:00 | 12:00 | 12:00 | |
| 1:00 | 1:00 | 1:00 | 1:00 | 1:00 | |
| 2:00 | 2:00 | 2:00 | 2:00 | 2:00 | SUNDAY ☐ |
| 3:00 | 3:00 | 3:00 | 3:00 | 3:00 | |
| 4:00 | 4:00 | 4:00 | 4:00 | 4:00 | |
| 5:00 | 5:00 | 5:00 | 5:00 | 5:00 | |
| 6:00 | 6:00 | 6:00 | 6:00 | 6:00 | |
| 7:00 | 7:00 | 7:00 | 7:00 | 7:00 | |

| Do. Call | Do. Call | Do. Call | Do. Call | Do. Call | Do. Call |
|---|---|---|---|---|---|
| | | | | | |

| $ Money in | $ Money in | $ Money in | $ Money in | $ Money in | $ Money in |
|---|---|---|---|---|---|
| | | | | | |

## Remembering Me

I am: _____

What I love about me is: _____

_____

What I am proud of this week is: _____

_____

## Weekly Goals:

1. _____ ○   3. _____ ○

2. _____ ○   4. _____ ○

## Not to Miss:

· _____   · _____

· _____   · _____

## Projects to Complete:

_____

_____

_____

_____

## Recipes to Try:

_____

_____

_____

## To Beautify my Home:

_____

_____

_____

## Call - Email - Social Media:

·           ·

·           ·

·           ·

·           ·

## To Do:

_____   _____

_____   _____

_____   ## Groceries:

_____   _____ ____

_____   _____ ____

_____   _____ ____

_____   _____ ____

## To Buy:

·           ·

·           ·

·           ·

*My Balanced Heart*

KIND KIN DEED
FAMILY HOLIDAY
COUPLES DATES
FRIENDS
HAVING FUN TOGETHER
MY FAMILY
BESTIES
SPOUSES FAMILY
KIND KID DEED
KIDS & PETS
SPOUSE
ALONE TIME
GROWING
ME
SELF CARE
MASSAGE
READING
WORK
CREATIVITY
SAVINGS
EXERCISE
SPIRITUAL WELL BEING
MUSIC
INVESTING
MEDITATION
CARDIO
WEIGHT
DEEP BREATHING
YOGA & STRETCHING
WALKING
TIME IN NATURE
CONTRIBUTING TO OTHERS

*My Weekly Reflection*

## What word best describes ME this week?

# Hey Psst... Don't Forget.

## Places to Uncover in This Big Beautiful World:

## To Buy:

## Recipes To Create:

## Blogs & Vlogs:

## Lent Out:

## YouTube Channels:

## Websites to Remember:

# Hey Psst... Don't Forget.

## My Bucket List:

_____    _____
_____    _____
_____    _____
_____    _____
_____    _____
_____    _____
_____    _____
_____

## Movies & Series to Watch:

_____    _____
_____    _____
_____    _____
_____    _____
_____    _____
_____    _____
_____    _____

## Restaurants to Devour:

_____    _____
_____    _____
_____    _____
_____    _____
_____    _____

## Songs to Enjoy:

·      ·
·      ·
·      ·
·      ·
·      ·
·      ·

## Books to Discover:

·      ·
·      ·
·      ·
·      ·
·      ·
·      ·

## Borrowed From:

·      ·
·      ·
·      ·
·      ·
·      ·

## Apps to Download:

·      ·
·      ·
·      ·
·      ·
·      ·
·      ·
·

# Project Brainstorm

**Project:**

_____

_____

_____

_____

**Project:**

_____

_____

_____

_____

**Project:**

_____

_____

_____

_____

**Project:**

_____

_____

_____

_____

**Project:**

_____

_____

_____

_____

**Project Brainstorm** A place to keep track of ideas, suggestions & random thoughts for your projects you want to complete this year. ♥

Project:

Project:

Project:

Project:

Project:

*Goals in writing are dreams with deadlines*

# My Exceptional Year ♥

January

_____
_____
_____
_____
_____
_____

February

_____
_____
_____
_____
_____
_____

March

_____
_____
_____
_____
_____
_____

April

_____
_____
_____
_____
_____
_____

May

_____
_____
_____
_____
_____
_____

June

_____
_____
_____
_____
_____
_____

July

_____
_____
_____
_____
_____
_____

August

_____
_____
_____
_____
_____
_____

September

_____
_____
_____
_____
_____
_____

October

_____
_____
_____
_____
_____
_____

November

_____
_____
_____
_____
_____
_____

December

_____
_____
_____
_____
_____
_____

# Summing the Year Up

| | MONEY IN | SAVINGS | SHARING WITH OTHERS | INSURANCE + HEALTH EXPENSES | HOUSE EXPENSES | GROCERIES | TRANSPORTATION EXPENSES | ENTERTAINMENT + FUN EXPENSES | HOLIDAY EXPENSES | PERSONAL EXPENSES | DINING OUT | MISC |
|---|---|---|---|---|---|---|---|---|---|---|---|---|
| JANUARY | | | | | | | | | | | | |
| FEBRUARY | | | | | | | | | | | | |
| MARCH | | | | | | | | | | | | |
| APRIL | | | | | | | | | | | | |
| MAY | | | | | | | | | | | | |
| JUNE | | | | | | | | | | | | |
| JULY | | | | | | | | | | | | |
| AUGUST | | | | | | | | | | | | |
| SEPTEMBER | | | | | | | | | | | | |
| OCTOBER | | | | | | | | | | | | |
| NOVEMBER | | | | | | | | | | | | |
| DECEMBER | | | | | | | | | | | | |
| $ TOTALS | | | | | | | | | | | | |

# Quick Reference

| A B C D | E F G H | I J K L |
|---------|---------|---------|

**A B C D**

NAME:
CONTACT:

NAME:
CONTACT:

NAME:
CONTACT:

NAME:
CONTACT:

NAME:
CONTACT:

NAME:
CONTACT:

NAME:
CONTACT:

NAME:
CONTACT:

NAME:
CONTACT:

NAME:
CONTACT:

NAME:
CONTACT:

NAME:
CONTACT:

NAME:
CONTACT:

**E F G H**

NAME:
CONTACT:

NAME:
CONTACT:

NAME:
CONTACT:

NAME:
CONTACT:

NAME:
CONTACT:

NAME:
CONTACT:

NAME:
CONTACT:

NAME:
CONTACT:

NAME:
CONTACT:

NAME:
CONTACT:

NAME:
CONTACT:

NAME:
CONTACT:

NAME:
CONTACT:

**I J K L**

NAME:
CONTACT:

NAME:
CONTACT:

NAME:
CONTACT:

NAME:
CONTACT:

NAME:
CONTACT:

NAME:
CONTACT:

NAME:
CONTACT:

NAME:
CONTACT:

NAME:
CONTACT:

NAME:
CONTACT:

NAME:
CONTACT:

NAME:
CONTACT:

NAME:
CONTACT:

# Quick Reference

| MNOP | QRST | UVWXYZ |
|---|---|---|

**MNOP**

NAME: _____
CONTACT: _____

NAME: _____
CONTACT: _____

NAME: _____
CONTACT: _____

NAME: _____
CONTACT: _____

NAME: _____
CONTACT: _____

NAME: _____
CONTACT: _____

NAME: _____
CONTACT: _____

NAME: _____
CONTACT: _____

NAME: _____
CONTACT: _____

NAME: _____
CONTACT: _____

NAME: _____
CONTACT: _____

NAME: _____
CONTACT: _____

NAME: _____
CONTACT: _____

NAME: _____
CONTACT: _____

**QRST**

NAME: _____
CONTACT: _____

NAME: _____
CONTACT: _____

NAME: _____
CONTACT: _____

NAME: _____
CONTACT: _____

NAME: _____
CONTACT: _____

NAME: _____
CONTACT: _____

NAME: _____
CONTACT: _____

NAME: _____
CONTACT: _____

NAME: _____
CONTACT: _____

NAME: _____
CONTACT: _____

NAME: _____
CONTACT: _____

NAME: _____
CONTACT: _____

NAME: _____
CONTACT: _____

NAME: _____
CONTACT: _____

**UVWXYZ**

NAME: _____
CONTACT: _____

NAME: _____
CONTACT: _____

NAME: _____
CONTACT: _____

NAME: _____
CONTACT: _____

NAME: _____
CONTACT: _____

NAME: _____
CONTACT: _____

NAME: _____
CONTACT: _____

NAME: _____
CONTACT: _____

NAME: _____
CONTACT: _____

NAME: _____
CONTACT: _____

NAME: _____
CONTACT: _____

NAME: _____
CONTACT: _____

NAME: _____
CONTACT: _____

NAME: _____
CONTACT: _____

# This Year's Joyful Journey

♥

Made in the USA
Charleston, SC
25 September 2016